For: Donna
God ... always!
Lucy Adams
Psalm 100:1

52

HYMN STORY
DEVOTIONS

Lucy Neeley Adams

Abingdon Press
Nashville

52 Hymn Story Devotions

This book is printed on acid-free, recycled paper.

ISBN 0-687-07807-5

To Jesus, my Lord and Savior,
to whom I sing praises.

"Holy, holy, holy is the Lord
God Almighty, who was, and is, and is to come."
(Rev. 4:8*b*, NIV)

06 07 08 09 — 10 9 8 7

MANUFACTURED IN THE UNITED STATES OF AMERICA

INTRODUCTION

The stories you are about to read represent much more than a brief insight into history. They are love stories. They reveal the most essential relationship in life—a loving response to God's love.

The hearts of countless men and women have been filled with that love. Evangelist and author Robert Tuttle, Jr., writes in his book, *Sanctity Without Starch:* "I've just finished rereading Chronicles I and II only to be reminded once again of just how crucial music is to the worship of God. Music gathers the people and pleases God. 'Hezekiah assigned the priests and Levites to divisions . . . As the offering began, singing to the LORD began also, accompanied by trumpets and the instruments of David, king of Israel. The whole assembly bowed in worship, while the singers sang and the trumpeters played' (2 Chron. 31:2; 29:27-28)."

Turning to the New Testament, we see that God's love flowed in a fresh and vibrant way into the original twelve disciples, who answered Jesus' call to follow him. The Gospel accounts in Matthew 26:30 and Mark 14:26 tell us that after the Last Supper, "when they had sung the hymn, they went out to the Mount of Olives." The accounts of the Resurrection and Pentecost are joyful pictures of the ever-loving and ever-living Jesus Christ, who will never leave us or forsake us. The world has been invaded by the fresh wind of the Spirit of God.

Throughout our hymnals, we see words and music from people who were inspired to write through their joys and sorrows. Through their stories they show that they were "not ashamed of the gospel, because it is the power of God for the salvation of everyone who believes" (Rom. 1:16 NIV). When first written, these hymns were contemporary to that time. They continue to be meaningful since "Jesus Christ is the same yesterday and today and forever" (Heb. 13:8). He is the reason I have written this book.

Lucy Neeley Adams

ACKNOWLEDGMENTS

Special appreciation is offered for the following:

- ♫ My loving husband Woody, who has patiently endured my long hours of study and writing;
- ♫ Our beloved children, John, Scott, Ben, and Joy, whose dear families bless us;
- ♫ The sponsors and producers at radio stations, who have broadcast my program, "The Story Behind the Song," since 1984;
- ♫ The Cookeville Creative Writers, who listen, affirm, and strengthen my writing abilities;
- ♫ Charles Denning, Executive Editor of the *Herald-Citizen*, in Cookeville, Tennessee, where my column, "SongStories," is published;
- ♫ Robert Tuttle, Jr., who read the manuscript and gave encouragement and valuable suggestions;
- ♫ My friend Cindie Miller, who edited, typed, and retyped each story I wrote;
- ♫ The wonderful authors listed in the Bibliography, without whom I would have no stories;
- ♫ Dr. Evelyn Laycock, who gave me peace about my book;
- ♫ Aldersgate Renewal Ministry for enriching my spiritual growth;
- ♫ Dr. John Abney, who helps me hear God's call on my life; and
- ♫ Mary Byrd King, who gave her proofreading skills.

CONTENTS

1. A MIGHTY FORTRESS IS OUR GOD

"God is our refuge and strength, a very present help in trouble." (Ps. 46:1)

A stormy conflict began on October 31, 1517, in Wittenberg, Germany, when a Catholic priest made a list of complaints against the church and nailed that list to the door of the Cathedral of Wittenberg.

That expression of anguish in the heart of Martin Luther ignited the greatest upheaval in centuries within the church. Much conflict arose between those who wanted change and those who did not. Fearing for Martin Luther's safety, a sympathetic friend led him to the shelter of a castle. It was there that Luther experienced afresh the protection and comfort of a mighty God. Within his temporary hiding place, God's Word became more alive and vibrant for him.

During those days of solitude, prayer, and Bible study, Luther began a translation of the Scriptures from Latin into German. "All people must be able to read God's word for themselves," he said. Only the priests were allowed to read the Bible at that time.

Luther also believed that congregational singing should be allowed. "The devil, who is the originator of sorrowful anxieties and restless troubles, flees before the sound of God's music almost as much as before the Word of God," Luther observed. With that inspiration, he composed the hymn "A Mighty Fortress Is Our God." Inspired by Psalm 46, it is a bold affirmation of a powerful and loving God.

When he returned to face his critics, Luther was armed with renewed determination that he would not recant his protests against the Roman Catholic Church. So, after a struggle for several years with officials in Rome, he was excommunicated in 1521.

However, this great Christian leader did not lose heart. He continued teaching and preaching the gospel of Jesus Christ until his death in 1546 at the age of sixty-three in the town of his birth, Eisleben, Saxony, Germany. This majestic hymn was sung at his funeral, and the first line is engraved on his tombstone.

In spite of Luther's excommunication, his hymn was accepted into the Roman Catholic Church in the 1960s. There are divisions in the church today, but this hymn unifies all believers in the love and the purposes of our God.

O God, your strength is my fortress and you are the same from age to age. What a blessing! In Jesus' name. Amen.

A mighty fortress is our God, a bulwark never failing;
our helper he amid the flood of mortal ills prevailing.
For still our ancient foe doth seek to work us woe;
his craft and power are great, and armed with cruel hate,
on earth is not his equal.

Martin Luther, ca. 1529; trans. by Frederick H. Hedge, 1853 (Ps. 46)

2. ABIDE WITH ME

"Stay with us, for it is nearly evening: the day is almost over." (Luke 24:29, NIV)

The fascinating story of two discouraged followers of Jesus walking on the road to Emmaus is the text for the memorable hymn "Abide with Me." The Crucifixion had shaken these two to their very souls. All hope was gone. They thought Jesus would be on earth forever. But he was gone.

When the risen Lord appeared to walk by their side, they did not recognize him. Upon reaching their home, they invited the stranger to stay and eat. As he blessed the bread and broke it, they realized who the stranger really was, and they ran out to tell the news to the disciples.

To discover that Jesus is alive is the turning point for every Christian. Henry Francis Lyte had experienced that revelation and felt the call to preach the gospel. Born in Scotland in 1793, he was ordained into the Church of England and went to serve the coastal village of Brixham. His faith grew strong although he was frail of body. Asthma and other lung disorders interfered with his ministry: eventually he was advised to leave the damp climate of his parish. But the thought of leaving the congregation he had served for twenty-four years grieved him. Before he even reached his new home in Italy, he died.

The parishioners in England grieved. They remembered

their pastor's last Sunday with them. He had expressed his faith in Jesus Christ and his assurance of eternal life. His daughter has written: "In the evening of that same day [September 4, 1847] he placed in the hands of a near and dear relative the little hymn, 'Abide with Me,' with the air of his own composing, adapted to the words."

In the second stanza the theme quickly changes from the scene on the road to Emmaus with Jesus to the thought that life passes by swiftly. This is a reality for everyone. I recognize that each passing day moves me closer to that moment when "earth's joys grow dim, its glories pass away."

The remainder of this prayer hymn is a beautiful testimony of what the Christian can expect when death becomes imminent. When the cross of Christ is held "before my closing eyes," I know that he will "shine through the gloom and point me to the skies."

O God, thank you for this dimension of your love. We continue to abide in you, whether on earth or in heaven. Amen.

Abide with me; fast falls the eventide;
the darkness deepens; Lord, with me abide.
When other helpers fail and comforts flee,
Help of the helpless, O abide with me.

Henry F. Lyte, 1847 (Luke 24:29)

3. ALL HAIL THE POWER OF JESUS' NAME

"Signs and wonders are performed through the name of your holy servant Jesus." (Acts 4:30)

If the Christian had just one anthem of praise, this would be it. In every nation where it is sung, it speaks to the deep spiritual needs of all. Someone has said, "As long as there are

Christians on earth, this hymn will continue to be sung, and after that—in heaven."

The composer of the hymn was Edward Perronet, who was born in Sundridge, England, in 1726. He was the son of a priest of the Church of England, and he, too, was ordained into that church. Young Perronet, however, felt the church cold and too formal, and began to work with two Anglican priests, John and Charles Wesley, who were experiencing the same struggle. They preached in the streets. Soon many people who were searching for a deeper faith gathered in the open air to hear the fiery evangelists.

The trio faced much persecution from those who disagreed with their ministry, sometimes even the threat of physical harm. John Wesley wrote in his diary: "Today Edward Perronet was thrown down and rolled in mud and mire."

But out of those times of distress came Perronet's powerful testimony of praise: "All hail the power of Jesus' name!" That same power flowed into the lives of true believers in the early church. Recorded in Acts 3 is the first miracle after Pentecost. The healing of the lame man at the temple caused an uproar from the Jewish leaders who watched the miracle. Peter, full of the Holy Spirit, said, "In the name of Jesus Christ of Nazareth, stand up and walk" (Acts 3:6). Instantly, the man leaped to his feet. The rulers and elders of the Jews, fearing this message would spread as a result of this miracle, commanded the disciples "not to speak or teach at all in the name of Jesus" (Acts 4:18).

The disciples did not obey this order, but continued to preach in that powerful Name. The results are astounding, as the gospel message has spread to millions throughout the centuries.

Lord Jesus, we crown you Lord of all. Hallelujah. Amen.

All hail the power of Jesus' name!
Let angels prostrate fall;
bring forth the royal diadem,
and crown him Lord of all.
Bring forth the royal diadem,
and crown him Lord of all.

Edward Perronet, 1779; alt. by John Rippon, 1787

4. Amazing Grace

"And God is able to make all grace abound to you."
(2 Cor. 9:8a, NIV)

Even the sound is sweet—grace, grace—it is amazing. Who wrote the words about grace that hundreds of years later are sung around the world?

He was just a little boy of seven when his mother died. Life in 1732 London, England, had been difficult for the young mother and her child. His father was a captain on a slave trading ship and was seldom with them. For those first seven years, the little boy was nurtured in the Christian faith because of his mother's loving guidance.

"Train a child in the way he should go, and when he is old he will not turn from it" (Prov. 22:6, NIV). This describes the early education of John Newton, composer of the beloved hymn "Amazing Grace."

After his mother's death and several years of living with relatives, John joined his father aboard ship. Captain Newton was a different influence from what John had known in his formative years. Daily, John witnessed cruel and harsh treatment toward the natives of West Africa who had been forced from their homes and sold as slaves. He grew hard and cold in this environment, and became a sailor whose goal was power, his motivation greed.

There were years of this degrading life before John Newton experienced a major turning point. During a severe storm at sea, he recognized his inadequacy in the face of death. Fear gripped him and he prayed to be spared. The sea eventually calmed. John Newton's inner life also had a new calmness and peace as he began to care for those he had once despised. Eventually he abandoned the life of the slave-trading ship. Hearing God's call to ministry, he entered seminary and was ordained into the Church of England. When he was thirty-nine years old, he began his preaching and music ministry. Of the many hymns he wrote, "Amazing Grace" is the one favored by millions.

John Newton died at the age of eighty-two. Before he left this earth, he was heard to say, "My memory is nearly gone, but I remember two things: I am a great sinner and Christ is a great Savior."

O God, I gratefully receive your loving gift of pardon. It is amazing. Amen.

Amazing grace!
How sweet the sound
that saved a wretch like me!
I once was lost, but now am found;
was blind, but now I see.

John Newton, 1779; st. 6 anon.

5. AMERICA THE BEAUTIFUL

"Blessed is the nation whose God is the LORD." (Ps. 33:12, NIV)

Our voices united in songs of patriotism at the close of the Fourth of July concert. Then the annual fireworks display began. But the distant strains of concert music lingered long in my heart even during the fireworks. One of my favorites, "America the Beautiful," never fails to lift my spirit. Heartfelt words express thankfulness that we live in a great and free country.

The poet, Katharine Lee Bates, chose to begin her poem by exclaiming, "O beautiful." With that opening, she unfolds many word pictures that capture the imagination.

While standing at the top of Pikes Peak near Colorado Springs, Colorado, in the summer of 1893, she was inspired to write this poem. In her journal she wrote: "It was there, as I was looking out over the sea-like expanse of fertile country, that the opening lines of this text formed themselves in my mind."

Bates, who was on a teaching assignment for the summer, was a native of New England. Born in Falmouth, Massachusetts, in 1859, the daughter of a minister, she began to write poetry during her childhood. Her education toward a teaching profession led her to Wellesley College.

Although she wrote this poem to describe the natural beauty

of this land, she also recognized the needs of all people to live in unity, self-control, and nobility. She believed these great desires could result only from the guidance of God in individual lives.

The poem was filed away in her notes for ten years while she revised and reworked it. When she submitted it to the editor of the *Boston Evening Transcript* in 1904, it was published and received with wide acclaim.

America at its finest is embodied in this song that asks for God's grace. Katharine Bates described it best when she said: "We must match the greatness of our country with the goodness of personal, godly living. If only we could couple the daring of the Pilgrims with the moral teachings of Moses, we would have something in this country that no one could ever take from us."

Thankfully, we have not been in danger of losing America. But how safe are the American values of righteousness and unity? Daniel Webster once said, "Whatever makes people good Christians makes them good citizens."

O God, mend our every flaw. Confirm our souls in self-control and our liberty in law. Amen.

O beautiful for spacious skies, for amber waves of grain;
for purple mountain majesties above the fruited plain!
America! America! God shed his grace on thee,
and crown thy good with brotherhood
from sea to shining sea.

Katharine Lee Bates, 1904

6. THE BATTLE HYMN OF THE REPUBLIC

"What does the LORD require of you but to do justice, and to love kindness, and to walk humbly with your God?" (Mic. 6:8)

The music was good. The words were horrible. The song that was sung that day in the summer of 1861 was a symbol of bloodshed and hate. "John Brown's body lay a-mouldering in the grave" was typical of the horrors of the Civil War. John Brown desired freedom for the slaves. The Southern and Northern states were bitterly opposed and thousands lay dead before the war was over. The descriptive message of the song was a warning.

But to some people it was repulsive. One of those was Julia Ward Howe, who stood watching the soldiers march by as they sang this song. Her husband and their pastor stood with her. They all agreed that there needed to be something better for people to sing. The pastor, Rev. James Freeman Clarke, suggested to Howe that she write some "decent words for that tune."

She said she would try. Little did she know that in only a few hours inspiring words would come to her, and eventually to the world through publication. They fit the melody that the soldiers had sung.

We have the personal background of this song because of a journal entry: "I awoke in the grey of the morning, and as I lay waiting for dawn, the long lines of the desired poem began to entwine themselves in my mind, and I said to myself, 'I must get up and write these verses, lest I fall asleep and forget them!' So I sprang out of bed and in the dimness found an old stump of a pen. . . . I scrawled the verses almost without looking at the paper."

From the first line to the end, I believe Julia Howe experienced the glory of the Lord. How else can we explain the speed with which she wrote, and the graphic images the song brings to mind? "The Lord is coming . . . he is trampling . . . his truth is marching. . . . He is sifting out the heart." She even reminds herself: "Be swift my soul to answer him!"

The story is told of Abraham Lincoln, who was so overjoyed when he heard this beautiful song at a political rally, he shouted out, "Sing it again!" The choir quickly fulfilled the request from the President and repeated this beautiful message: "Mine eyes have seen the glory of the coming of the Lord."

For more than a century, we have continued to be inspired by this unforgettable melody with its words of triumph.

Lord, you were born "across the sea" and also in me. I behold your glory. Amen.

Mine eyes have seen the glory of the coming of the Lord;
he is trampling out the vintage where the grapes
of wrath are stored;

he hath loosed the fateful lightning of his terrible swift sword;
his truth is marching on.

Refrain: Glory, glory, hallelujah! Glory, glory, hallelujah!
Glory, glory, hallelujah! His truth is marching on.

Julia Ward Howe, 1861, sts. 1-4; st. 5, anon.

7. BENEATH THE CROSS OF JESUS

"For the message of the cross is foolishness to those who
are perishing." (1 Cor. 1:18*a*, NIV)

Elizabeth Cecilia Clephane was raised in the small village
of Melrose, among the rolling hills of Scotland. She was born
in Edinburgh in 1830. Frail and sickly most of her life,
Elizabeth was blessed with a loving spirit and a cheerful dispo-
sition, which inspired her village friends to give her an endear-
ing nickname, "the sunbeam."

Elizabeth and her sisters helped the needy in their village.
She did what she could within her limitations. A devoted student of the Bible, she expressed her faith in the form of poetry;
her testimony is one of enduring strength.

"Beneath the Cross of Jesus" was written in 1868, just one
year before her death at the age of thirty-nine. The first verse
includes symbolism from the Old Testament: "A mighty rock"
(Isa. 32:2); "the weary land" (Ps. 63:1); "home within the
wilderness" (Jer. 9:2); "rest upon the way" (Isa. 28:12); and
"the noontide heat" (Isa. 4:6). The "burden of the day" is
taken from Matthew 11:30 in the New Testament.

As Paul writes to the Christians in Corinth, the cross does
seem like foolishness to those who do not understand its necessity.
As I "take my stand" beneath it, I imagine the blood flowing from
my Savior. The second verse affirms: "Mine eyes at times can see
the very dying form of One who suffered there for me."

The suffering of crucifixion was cruel, but within that act,
God planned for the redemption of the world. Faith in that
blood cleanses all from their sin.

I have a beautiful wooden statue of Jesus the Christ carrying his cross. The cross can be lifted from his arms. I have often thought that this statue is a symbol of the way I relate to a burden I may have to carry. I want relief; I want to be rid of the burden. But I know that Jesus lovingly bears this burden with me, as he says, "My yoke is easy and my burden is light."

Lord Jesus, from your cradle, to your cross, to your risen presence, I rejoice in the "wonders of your glorious love." Amen.

Beneath the cross of Jesus
I fain would take my stand,
the shadow of a mighty rock
within a weary land;
a home within the wilderness,
a rest upon the way,
from the burning of the noontide heat,
and the burden of the day.

Elizabeth C. Clephane, 1872

8. BLESSED ASSURANCE

"Our gospel did not come to you in word only, but also in power . . . and in much assurance." (1 Thess. 1:5, NKJV)

It was a casual visit to see a friend that day in 1873. But a great moment in church music was about to occur.

When Fanny Crosby entered her friend's home, Phoebe Knapp was playing beautiful music at the organ. "What does that melody say to you, Fanny?" Fanny thought for a moment and then the words of "Blessed Assurance" came from deep within her heart.

That was the way many of Fanny Crosby's poems were written—quickly. This woman, blind from childhood, wrote the words to more than eight thousand hymns in her lifetime of ninety-five years. Leading musicians often asked her for lyrics for their compositions.

Although she never wrote the music for the hymns that bear her name, she was a very gifted musician. She played the guitar and harp. Her faith was a joyful experience and quite humbling, especially when she sang many of the hymns she had written.

In the hymn "Blessed Assurance," her personal relationship with Jesus Christ is revealed. On November 20, 1850, at a camp meeting, Fanny experienced a profound deepening of her faith: "I felt my very soul was flooded with celestial light. For the first time I realized that I had been trying to hold the world in one hand and the Lord in another."

"From that moment on," she said, "the words I wrote were a song of the heart addressed to God."

Like Fanny Crosby, I experience a continual spiritual juggling act. It is tiring to live with the demands of each day in one hand and the desire to focus and serve the Lord in the other.

This dilemma is explained in a humorous way by authors Ray and Anne Ortland. They say, "The temptations that really sap our spiritual power are the television, banana cream pie, the easy chair, and the credit card. The Christian wins or loses in those seemingly innocent moments of decision."

However, God has made it possible to "approach with a true heart in full assurance of faith" (Heb. 10:22). The words of this beautiful hymn remind us that assurance is a "foretaste of glory divine."

O God, thank you for the knowledge that you are always near me. I am secure in that promise. In Jesus' name. Amen.

Blessed assurance, Jesus is mine!
O what a foretaste of glory divine!
Heir of salvation, purchase of God,
born of his Spirit, washed in his blood.

Refrain: This is my story, this is my song,
praising my Savior all the day long;
this is my story, this is my song,
praising my Savior all the day long.

Fanny J. Crosby, 1873

9. Blest Be the Tie That Binds

"By this [love] everyone will know that you are my disciples, if you have love for one another." (John 13:35)

Life was good for Rev. and Mrs. John Fawcett. Within their small Baptist church in Wainsgate, Yorkshire, England, there were loving Christians who listened to sermons, prayed prayers, and sang hymns. It was an ideal place for ministry for a young preacher and his wife. They were very content.

But one day in 1772 an invitation came from a church in London for Fawcett to come and be their pastor. It was a larger, more prestigious church with an increase in salary. Everything indicated that this would be a very good move. The decision was made. They packed their belongings and said their farewells. Fawcett preached his final sermon at the little church.

Then the unexpected happened. Reverend Fawcett changed his mind. The tie that bound him to this small parish was too strong: his parishoners' sorrow and unembarrassed tears convinced him to stay. He remained there for fifty-four years.

History records that "Blest Be the Tie That Binds" may have been a direct response to the expressions of love from his congregation during that one short time of indecision.

When I sing the third stanza, I remember friends who will always be loved because "we share each other's woes, our mutual burdens bear; and often for each other flows the sympathizing tear." Caring love can be expressed with words, but often is expressed with tears.

The story is told of little Billy, who sat on the sidewalk curb with his friends. Since they were all crying, a friend stopped to ask what was wrong. One little boy replied, "We've got a pain in Billy's stomach." Billy will never forget the friends who helped him cry. That is the tie that binds our hearts in everlasting love—God's kind of love.

Lord, help me to be spontaneous with love. Nudge me when you see a need, and flow through me. Amen.

Blest be the tie that binds
our hearts in Christian love;
the fellowship of kindred minds
is like to that above.

John Fawcett, 1782

10. CHRIST THE LORD IS RISEN TODAY

"Go quickly and tell his disciples, 'He has been raised from the dead.' " (Matt. 28:7)

This majestic hymn brings a smile to my face as I joyfully sing it and proclaim the central belief of the Christian faith. Without this truth we would have only a history of a man named Jesus. Charles Wesley wrote these words to tell the Good News: Jesus died, but was raised from the dead and remains alive through the power of the Holy Spirit.

Charles's life was steeped in this knowledge. Born in Epworth, England in 1707, he was raised in a Christian home and taught the scriptures by his mother. He graduated from Oxford University and was ordained a priest in the Church of England.

Charles and his brother John were sent to America by the church to evangelize the Indians. After a year in the New World, Charles returned to England. John followed a year later. During this time, Charles felt restless. His spiritual life was empty.

But on Sunday, May 21, 1738, Charles was touched by the fire of the Holy Spirit. He wrote in his journal: "At nine my brother and some friends came and sang a hymn to the Holy Ghost. . . . In about half an hour they went. I betook myself to prayer. Yet still the Spirit of God strove with my own and the evil spirit till by degrees He chased away the darkness of my unbelief. I found myself convinced and fell into intercession."

From that moment on Charles Wesley was as bold in his witness as the disciples were after Pentecost. Jesus had told them "You will receive power when the Holy Spirit has come upon you; and you will be my witnesses" (Acts 1:8). Charles's emptiness was gone. In its place was a consuming fire that eventually ignited much of England. The people called Methodists were birthed from this fervor. More than 6,500 hymns were written by this dynamic musical genius.

"Christ the Lord Is Risen Today" was written in 1739, one year after Charles Wesley's spiritual baptism. His heart for the gospel is reflected in the words and music.

Never have I been so moved as when I sang this hymn, along with four different church choirs, one Easter Sunday in Murfreesboro, Tennessee. As our voices rose, united in sharing the glorious message, I was touched by the fire that consumed Charles Wesley—the fire of joy. Christ is risen!

O God, you raised Jesus, and you gave us the Holy Spirit. I thank you for that abundant life. In his name. Amen.

Christ the Lord is risen today, Alleluia!
Earth and heaven in chorus say, Alleluia!
Raise your joys and triumphs high, Alleluia!
Sing, ye heavens, and earth reply, Alleluia!

Charles Wesley, 1739

11. COME, YE THANKFUL PEOPLE, COME

"Make a joyful noise to the LORD, all the earth. . . . Enter his gates with thanksgiving." (Ps. 100:1, 4*a*)

Teenagers make many plans in their journey toward adulthood, many of which never transpire. When Henry Alford was only sixteen years old, he wrote a profound promise in the front of his Bible: "I do this day, in the presence of God and my own soul, renew my covenant with God and solemnly determine henceforth to become His, and to do His work as far as in me lies."

Alford was born in London, England, on October 7, 1810. He was nurtured by Christian parents and greatly influenced by a grandfather and father who were Anglican clergymen. Their example led to his personal commitment to Jesus Christ. Alford lived up to the promise he made as a teenager: his life was a testimony to Christian commitment. Upon graduation from Trinity College, Cambridge, he began his ministry as theologian, poet, and musician. Dr. Alford was eventually appointed dean of Canterbury Cathedral, known as the "mother church" of England. His death in 1871 left a void in the hearts of many people whom God had touched through his ministry.

Alford's pen, however, left the world with the memorable hymn of thanksgiving, "Come, Ye Thankful People, Come." Written in 1844, the hymn's purpose was to help celebrate the times of harvest festival in the English countryside. It is an invitation to join the festivities in loving response to a faithful God. It is also a tribute to Alford's life.

Two stanzas summarize Jesus' parable of the wheat and tares in Matthew 13. The hymn closes with a prayer that anticipates Jesus' second coming: "Lord . . . gather thou thy people in, free from sorrow, free from sin."

A thankful heart is pleasing to God. Since the beginning of America's history, governors and presidents have declared the necessity of a special day to give thanks. But a specific day was not officially set until 1941, when Congress voted that each fourth Thursday in November would be an official holiday of Thanksgiving.

We have a thousand things pulling us in different directions every day. But on Thanksgiving Day, I try not to let things like cooking and television distract me, because I want to focus on giving thanks to the Source of all blessings.

Dear God, I am thankful that "this is the day that the Lord has made; we will rejoice and be glad in it." Amen.

Come, ye thankful people, come, raise the song
of harvest home;
all is safely gathered in, ere the winter storms begin.

God our Maker doth provide for our wants to be supplied;
come to God's own temple, come, raise the song
of harvest home.

Henry Alford, 1844, alt. (Mark 4:26-29; Matt. 13:36-43)

12. DAY IS DYING IN THE WEST

"O give thanks to the Lord. . . . who made the great lights, . . .
the sun to rule over the day, . . . the moon and stars to rule over
the night." (Ps. 136:3*a*, 7*a*, 8*a*, 9*a*)

In the late afternoon, the sky turns from pale pink to deep
red, with a splash of purple thrown in. When the day is over
and darkness covers the world, the moon and stars become
beautiful reminders of even more of God's glorious creation.

The hymn "Day Is Dying in the West" captures this beauty in words and music. Author Mary Lathbury was inspired
by the sunset on Lake Chautauqua near Jamestown, New
York. Those were hallowed grounds in 1877 to the people who
attended Christian retreats there. Lathbury, a beloved and
respected leader at the conferences, was known as the "Poet
Laureate and Saint of Chautauqua."

She was born in 1841 in Manchester, New York into a family of clergy. Mary, an art teacher, also felt God's call on her life.
Her consecration is evident in the words of "Day Is Dying in
the West." Great moments of worship are expressed in the chorus, "Holy, holy, holy, Lord God of Hosts . . . Heaven and earth
are praising thee." These words rest on beautiful music composed by William Sherwin, music director at Lake Chautauqua.

The second stanza affirms God's desire to "gather us who
seek thy face to the fold of thy embrace." The blessed security
of that loving embrace was evident in the Rodgers family when
their daughter, Mary Lee, was born on August 16, 1998. She
had multiple problems at birth and lived for only nineteen
days. My husband, Woody, and I rushed to their home in time
to join the tears and prayers of grieving loved ones.

Weeks later they wrote a letter of gratitude: "Mary Lee

entered our lives and entwined herself around our hearts like the tendrils of a morning glory. Her blooming was short yet beautiful. From her conception to her death, Mary Lee has broadened our understanding of God's love."

The last verse of the hymn speaks of those who die in Christ: "Lord of angels, on our eyes let eternal morning rise and shadows end." In Christ there is no more death, no more shadows, no more tears when we see the eternal sunrise.

O God, "Heaven and earth are full of thee, heaven and earth are praising thee, O Lord most high." Amen.

Day is dying in the west;
heaven is touching earth with rest;
wait and worship while the night
sets the evening lamps alight
through all the sky.

Refrain: Holy, holy, holy, Lord God of Hosts!
Heaven and earth are full of thee! Heaven and earth
are praising thee,
O Lord most high!

Mary A. Lathbury, 1878 (Isa. 6:3)

13. ETERNAL FATHER, STRONG TO SAVE

"My help comes from the LORD." (Ps. 121:2)

The crowd seemed breathless as the melody of this beautiful hymn was eloquently played by the Navy Band. The day was crisp and clear in Washington, D.C., but the world was in grief. The death of John F. Kennedy two days before had brought the world to a stop. His casket was carried slowly up the steps of the Capitol. The following day, it was carried down those same steps as the body of a beloved leader departed the familiar building for the last time. The Marine Band played this stately hymn at the conclusion of the burial service at Arlington National Cemetery.

Another sad day in history was April 14, 1945. This hymn was the one chosen to be sung at the funeral of President Franklin D. Roosevelt. It had been his favorite.

The words are a prayer written in 1860 for the safety of a student in Southampton, England. The student was preparing to set sail for America, and the long journey on the Atlantic Ocean could be very dangerous. The author, William Whiting, was born in 1825 in London. For thirty-six years he was the headmaster of an institution that dated from 1382—Winchester College Choristers' School. The school is located only a few miles from a major seaport. Verse 3 refers to incidents of danger on the sea: "O hear us when we cry to thee, For those in peril on the sea."

A lasting tribute to this fine Christian leader, who died in 1878, is the prayer that he wrote, "Eternal Father, Strong to Save." It was immediately set to music and published in the highly regarded 1861 edition of the Anglican Church hymnal, *Hymns Ancient and Modern.* Additional verses were added for inclusion in the *Missionary Service Book of 1937.*

When Woody and I left San Francisco with our two young sons on February 20, 1962, our destination was Seoul, Korea, where we were to be missionaries. We felt secure on the huge ship, the *President Cleveland,* with the many prayers of our family and friends fresh in our hearts. That was the same day another American journeyed far beyond the boundaries of his country: astronaut John Glenn. Millions prayed for his safe return on that historic day and again, three decades later, when Senator Glenn journeyed back into space.

O God, because of you, I am safe and secure from all fear. Thank you. Amen.

Eternal Father, strong to save,
whose arm hath bound the restless wave,
who bidst the mighty ocean deep
its own appointed limits keep:
O hear us when we cry to thee
for those in peril on the sea.

William Whiting, 1861

24

14. Go, Tell It on the Mountain

"You who bring good tidings to Zion, go up on a high mountain. . . . Lift up your voice with a shout, . . . say to the towns of Judah, 'Here is your God!' " (Isa. 40:9, NIV)

The carolers in our town who sing from door to door often sound like a band of angels. One Christmas, in the midst of feverish preparations in the kitchen, I heard them on my front porch, singing one of my favorite hymns, "Go, Tell It on the Mountain."

"Go, Tell It on the Mountain" was printed in a 1907 publication by Thomas Fenner, *Original Folk Songs of the Negro as Sung on the Plantation*. It was then entitled "Christmas Plantation Song." The original verses have been deleted from modern hymnals.

Two verses were added by John W. Work, Jr., a history professor at Fisk University. His son, John W. Work, III, was the author of *American Negro Songs and Spirituals* (1940), which gives significant insights into the origins of the spirituals. He says, "Many of them were passed down from generation to generation, and after much singing, the texts and melodies varied from place to place. But the gospel message was always proclaimed."

The gospel message of Jesus is certainly proclaimed by those who sing this carol. We are reminded of his words in Matthew 28:19: "Go therefore and make disciples of all nations."

Our family will never forget the sermon my husband, Woody, preached on Christmas of 1994, "Where Does God Fit In?" A child had asked that question when he looked at the manger scene. He had heard that God did something wonderful at Christmas, but he didn't see God in the manger.

Our son-in-law Edward, a nonbeliever, shared with us the good news of the birth of Jesus in his own heart. He joyfully said, "Life will never be the same again. I saw Dad's enthusiasm as he preached. Now I understand where God fits in. He was in the manger—as baby Jesus."

We were reminded that thousands of years ago the prophet Isaiah said, "Lift up your voice with a shout! Say, 'Here is your God!' " The glorious message never changes.

Jesus, we will go and tell. In your precious name. Amen.

Refrain: Go, tell it on the mountain, over the hills and
everywhere;
go, tell it on the mountain, that Jesus Christ is born.

While shepherds kept their watching
o'er silent flocks by night,
behold throughout the heavens
there shone a holy light.

African American spiritual; adapt. by John W. Work, Jr., 1907
(Luke 2:8-20)

15. GOD WILL TAKE CARE OF YOU

"As for me and my household, we will serve the LORD."
(Josh. 24:15*b*)

Dr. W. Stillman Martin and his wife, Civilla, were an out-
standing evangelistic team, taking their ministry throughout
the United States at the turn of the twentieth century. He
preached, while she sang and led others in singing.

While visiting the campus at the Practical Bible Training
School in Lestershire, New York, in 1904, this special ministry
was interrupted temporarily when Civilla was struck with a
sudden illness. Torn between his commitment to preach and
his concern for his wife, Dr. Martin decided to remain with
her. "You're too ill to stay alone," he said. "I must stay with
you." "But Father," their young son interrupted, "don't you
think that if God wants you to preach today, He will take care
of Mother while you are away?"

Disconcerted, Dr. Martin heeded his son's words and kept
his appointment at the church that day. His son had given him
fresh insight into the promises of God. Of course God would be
present with his wife and care for her. How could he doubt it?

When he returned home, he was relieved to find Civilla
feeling much better. But her recovery was not all that awaited

him. While he was gone, Civilla had been inspired to write a very special poem, which she called "God Will Take Care of You." Imagine the little boy's happiness when he was told that his words had inspired his mother to write it. Imagine his parents' pride in their son, who trusted in God's loving care.

Dr. Martin immediately went to their reed organ to set the poem to music. The beautiful notes that flowed from his fingertips matched this message of hope and encouragement.

This is also a hymn of comfort. When I change the pronoun and say, "God will take care of *me*," I am reminded of Psalm 55:22: "Cast your cares on the LORD and he will sustain you." Within the four stanzas and the chorus that promise is affirmed ten times.

At times, I am the weary one in the last stanza who sings, "No matter what may be the test, . . . lean weary one, upon his breast." The Martin's son knew the truth of God's promises. Today, it is still a blessing to sing this hymn of childlike faith.

O God, as your love is shared it spreads to others. Help us to live in the knowledge that you will take care of us every day. Amen.

Be not dismayed whate'er betide,
God will take care of you;
beneath his wings of love abide,
God will take care of you.

Refrain: God will take care of you, through every day, o'er all the way; he will take care of you, God will take care of you.

Civilla D. Martin, 1904

16. HAVE THINE OWN WAY, LORD

"Just like the clay in the potter's hand, so are you in my hand, O house of Israel." (Jer. 18:6)

Out of discouragement and frustration often come beautiful hymns of surrender. So it was for Adelaide Pollard, born in

Bloomfield, Iowa in 1862. Feeling a direct call from God to go into missionary service, she prepared well for a teaching career. Adelaide felt led to the continent of Africa, but acquiring the needed funds did not seem possible.

Frustrated and weary, she attended a prayer meeting one night. It was a blessing to sit quietly and listen. The elderly woman who prayed out loud that night spoke to God with a sincere request of her own. But it was different from Pollard's prayer. Instead of pleading for her needs, this simple prayer was: "It really doesn't matter what you do with us, Lord, just have your way in our lives."

These words turned Adelaide Pollard's life around. She felt new peace and hope. Her prayers would be answered in God's way. When she returned home she opened her Bible to Jeremiah 18 and freshened her memory about the potter and the clay. This captivating symbol of God as Potter, molding her life of clay, took deep root in her spirit. The words came easily as she began to write a poem to express her deeper understanding of this concept. Other parts of the Bible, especially the Psalms, were inspirational as she wrote her prayer with these words, "Search me, try me, wash me, help me, touch me, heal me and fill me." Before she lay down that night in 1902, all four stanzas of "Have Thine Own Way" were written.

This prayer-hymn has a profound message because each word is a commitment. It should not be taken lightly. I'll never forget the day I got a new insight about this hymn. Hoping my young son would take an afternoon nap, I rocked him while singing, "Have Thine Own Way, Lord." When he didn't go to sleep, I left him in his room to rest.

I was exasperated as I left the room. In my imagination I pictured him singing, "Have MY own way, Lord, have MY own way." He got his way, too—no sleep. Then I remembered in that moment the many times when I have wanted my own way. It is easier to sing the beautiful hymn than to practice its message in daily life.

O God, you see my heart. Forgive me when it is crowded with my self-will. Amen.

Have thine own way, Lord! Have thine own way!
Thou art the potter; I am the clay.

Mold me and make me after thy will,
while I am waiting, yielded and still.

Adelaide A. Pollard, 1902 (Jer. 18:6)

17. HOLY, HOLY, HOLY!
LORD GOD ALMIGHTY

"Holy, holy, holy is the LORD of hosts; the whole earth is full of his glory!" (Isa. 6:3)

My church was beautiful to me as a little child. The stained glass windows surrounded wonderfully loving people. Sitting next to my mother made me feel very secure, and when we stood to sing the hymns I leaned on her arm. Feeling inadequate to join in the singing, I merely listened. I will never forget the majesty of one special hymn. It seemed to swirl around me and flow right into my soul.

The text of the hymn was beyond my understanding. But there was no mistaking the basic message. The Lord God Almighty is Holy! Now I understand the hymn's real message as one of the basic doctrines of the church. Embodied in its four verses are the attributes of the Trinity: "God in three persons, blessed Trinity."

It was a poem written for Trinity Sunday, which is the eighth Sunday after Easter. Its author, Reginald Heber, was born near Cheshire, England, in 1783. Educated at Oxford University, he was ordained into the Church of England in 1807. He was an eloquent preacher and a published writer of poetry, essays, and hymns. Wanting to find more suitable hymns for his people to sing in church, he wrote his own and compiled them into a hymnal in 1820. It was the first to be organized into topics for each Sunday in the church year.

Heber's superior, however, who was the Bishop in London, rejected the hymnal, saying, "The time is not ripe for such a book of worship." The Anglican Church continued to sing the same formal church music.

The vivacious and gifted minister was assigned to India as Bishop of Calcutta. After three strenuous years of leadership, he died. His premature death at the age of forty-three was a great loss to the church. The hymnal that had not been accepted prior to his death was published in his memory, and was eagerly received. Of the fifty-seven hymns it contained, the one best remembered is "Holy, Holy, Holy." It unites Christians worldwide as we sing about the vision of our heavenly home portrayed in Revelation. The deep meaning of Reginald Heber's song is etched on our minds as we read Revelation 4:8-11. This vision of the throne of God is the theme of this majestic hymn.

In reverence we worship the true and living God as we sing: "All thy works shall praise thy name, in earth and sky and sea. Only thou art holy; there is none beside thee."

Lord God, what a privilege to praise you. Help me to stay focused on your glory. Amen.

Holy, holy, holy! Lord God almighty!
Early in the morning our song shall rise to thee.
Holy, holy, holy! Merciful and mighty,
God in three persons, blessed Trinity!

Reginald Heber, 1826 (Rev. 4:8-11)

18. HOW FIRM A FOUNDATION

"For no one can lay any foundation other than the one that has been laid; that foundation is Jesus Christ." (1 Cor. 3:11)

We do not know who wrote this hymn. But when the composer of "How Firm a Foundation" finished life on this earth, I believe the words of Jesus in the parable of the talents in Matthew 25 rang out loud and clear. "Well done, good and faithful servant . . . enter into the joy of your Lord." Since the name of the composer is unknown, we thank God for this person who contributed such knowledge of the Bible to future generations. For this is truly a hymn of faith, and a bold affirmation of God's Word.

It was first printed in 1787 in a hymnal by John Rippon: *A Selection of Hymns from the Best Authors*. So we can assume that one of those "best authors," listed only as "K," was the composer of this hymn, which was first titled "Exceeding Great and Precious Promises."

Kenneth W. Osbeck focuses our attention on the reason that these "great precious promises" were written. He says: "A believer's stability in this life, as well as his confidence for eternity, rests solely on the written promises of God's Word. The direction of the living God for our lives is very definite. It is found in a firm foundation—the written revelation, 'Thus saith the Lord' " (*Amazing Grace*, p. 14).

From the first verse, we are reminded of God's promises. They are as bedrock truth. "What more can he say than to you he hath said, to you who for refuge to Jesus have fled?" The succeeding verses build on that foundation—excerpts from the Bible that reaffirm this composer's faith and are relevant for all times. The gifted writer "K" combined these beautifully into poetic form.

When I was a new student of my Bible, I stood in awe of the peace, comfort, and direction that I was finding as I read and reread its message. I know there is no magic cure in holding it, but for several heart-wrenching funeral services at our church, I held it securely in my hand. I needed God's words of hope. On the inside front cover, I wrote "Holding on to this at the funeral of Mark (1971), Linda (1972), Netia (1973), and Grady (1974)." An automobile accident, cancer, and a heart attack had taken these four special people from the earth. Tears flowed, but God comforted.

O God, thank you for your promise, "I'll never, no never, no never forsake you." You are my solid foundation. Amen.

How firm a foundation, ye saints of the Lord,
is laid for your faith in his excellent word!
What more can he say than to you he hath said,
to you who for refuge to Jesus have fled?

"K" in Rippon's *Selection of Hymns, 1787* (2 Tim. 2:19; Heb. 13:5; Isa. 43:1-2)

19. I AM THINE, O LORD

"Draw near to God, and he will draw near to you." (James 4:8*a*)

The hour was late, but the conversation was uplifting, so they continued to talk. Visiting the Doane family in Cincinnati, Ohio, was always a treat for Fanny Crosby. This particular visit in 1874 produced a hymn that has had an impact upon all who prayerfully read or sing it, even a century later.

"I Am Thine, O Lord" was conceived from a discussion about the nearness of God. The response is a personal commitment: "I long to rise in the arms of faith and be closer drawn to thee." Everyone must make a choice: Do I draw near or do I refuse?

For the musical team of Doane and Crosby, this choice had already been made. Their experience of that closeness to God was the inspiration for this hymn.

No doubt they talked about the Christian's desire to have a closer walk with the Lord—to seek his will, and to commune with him as friend to friend. In the midst of this discussion, Fanny Crosby spoke these words in poetic form. Through blind eyes she focused her spiritual sight upon the most essential relationship of life: accepting Jesus Christ as Lord and growing in the knowledge of his presence. The music that carries the message was composed by William Doane.

In the book, *Rise and Walk,* Dennis Byrd expresses his gratitude that, in the midst of a crisis, he knew the presence of his Lord. When a jolting tackle was made on the football field, it changed his life forever. The New York Jets star lay very still on the ground—he could feel nothing, he could not move. He says: "I had no idea what lay ahead of me, but I knew this was going to be a test, a trial in my life for which I would need God's help and a strong faith. And I believed I had both those things. I had spent my entire life reading the Bible, studying the scriptures, and learning about God and Jesus Christ."

The life of Dennis Byrd will never be the same. He speaks of the unknown future, but drawing close to his Lord before this tragedy was the key to overcoming despair. Hope arises within the soul whose security rests in the assurance of God's presence. Fanny Crosby expresses this in the second verse of this hymn: "Let my soul look up with a steadfast hope, and my will be lost in thine." God gives us hope.

O Lord, when I open my eyes every morning I want to sing this prayer for you, "I am thine, O Lord." Amen.

I am thine, O Lord, I have heard thy voice,
and it told thy love to me;
but I long to rise in the arms of faith
and be closer drawn to thee.

Refrain: Draw me nearer, nearer, blessed Lord, to the cross
where thou hast died.
Draw me nearer, nearer, nearer, blessed Lord,
to thy precious, bleeding side.

Fanny J. Crosby, 1875 (Heb. 10:22)

20. I LOVE TO TELL THE STORY

"For you will be his witness to all the world of what you have seen and heard." (Acts 22:15)

The girls in the class were eager to learn about the gospel. They had been taught well. Their enthusiastic teacher, Katherine Hankey, was a natural for such leadership because she herself had been a student of the gospel from childhood. Born in England in 1834, her family guided her in the faith. As members of the Anglican Church, they actively shared the gospel among the wealthy in their elite suburb of London. The evangelistic spirit, however, was moving rapidly among all classes of people. So it was fitting that Katherine, nicknamed Kate, would reach out to teach Sunday school classes among the poor as well as the rich.

At age thirty, Kate was taken ill and spent the time while in recovery writing poetry that told the story of Jesus. She organized this poetry into two sections entitled, "The Story Wanted" and "The Story Told." Each section had fifty verses. From the second section she condensed her thoughts into the hymn "I Love to Tell the Story." It fully covers Jesus' life, focusing on his glory and love but just touching on his birth, life, and Resurrection. It creates a desire to know more. New believers ask, "Who is Jesus? Where do I learn the details of his life?"

Isn't it encouraging to see Bible students who already know the story continue to come to study groups? Even after a lifetime of knowing Jesus, we still hunger and thirst to hear the story like new Christians. The last verse affirms this: "And when, in scenes of glory, I sing the new, new song, 'twill be the old, old story that I have loved so long."

I enjoy singing with the residents at a local nursing home. The songs we share vary from sacred oldies to golden oldies with memories that are entwined within the brain and heart.

One afternoon, Carrie Shook, who was one hundred years old, asked that I come by her room to visit. The tattered black leather Bible on her bedside offered witness that she had loved to hear the story for a long time. Her whispery voice repeated the words of several old hymns. What a joy to hear her say, "I like hearing about Jesus. He keeps me company all the time." My precious friend blessed my life that day.

Lord Jesus, help me to tell your story over and over and over again. In your name. Amen.

I love to tell the story of unseen things above,
of Jesus and his glory, of Jesus and his love.
I love to tell the story, because I know 'tis true,
it satisfies my longings as nothing else can do.

Refrain: I love to tell the story, 'twill be my theme in glory,
to tell the old, old story of Jesus and his love.

Katherine Hankey, ca. 1868

21. I Need Thee Every Hour

"My God will fully satisfy every need of yours according to his riches in glory in Christ Jesus." (Phil. 4:19)

Teenager Annie Sherwood was happy that her hometown newspaper in Hoosick, New York, printed her poetry. She was encouraged by such an affirmation of her dream to be a writer. Another encouragement came years later when her minister, musician Robert Lowry, asked to write music for her poems. Annie Sherwood Hawks, now married and living in Brooklyn, wrote about her experience that led to the writing of "I Need Thee Every Hour."

> One day as a young wife and mother of 37 years of age, I was busy with my regular household tasks. Suddenly, I became filled with the sense of nearness to the Master, and I began to wonder how anyone could ever live without Him, either in joy or pain. Then the words were ushered into my mind and these thoughts took full possession of me.

Within a few months this poem and its music, composed by Robert Lowry, was published for the National Baptist Sunday School Convention of 1872 in Cincinnati. When Hawks's husband died sixteen years later, she wrote: "I did not understand at first why this hymn had touched the great throbbing heart of humanity. It was not until long after, when the shadow fell over my way, the shadow of a great loss, that I understood something of the comforting power in the words."

When that difficult hour came for Annie Hawks, she had the strength in her spiritual life that carried her through the valley. Long before she experienced the grief of her husband's death, she had written: "I need thee every hour, in joy or pain. Come quickly and abide or life is vain."

The question comes to my mind: Am I aware of the presence of Jesus so that I can recognize his touch in my daily routines?

Lord Jesus, my deepest need is to stay connected to you. Amen.

I need thee every hour,
most gracious Lord;
no tender voice like thine
can peace afford.

Refrain: I need thee, O I need thee; every hour I need thee;
O bless me now, my Savior, I come to thee.

Annie S. Hawks, 1872 (John 15:5)

22. IN THE GARDEN

"You are looking for Jesus of Nazareth, who was crucified. He has been raised; he is not here." (Mark 16:6)

God so loved the world that he sent Jesus, but when he was crucified, it seemed that God's plan was defeated. Behold the risen Lord! He is alive and millions have believed since that event.

One of those believers was C. Austin Miles. Born in Lakehurst, New Jersey, in 1868, he studied to be a pharmacist but returned to an earlier interest in music. When someone asked him to write a hymn "that brings hope to the hopeless and rest for the weary," he turned in his Bible to his favorite passage—John 20. The composer wrote:

> I seemed to be a part of the scene. I became a silent witness to that dramatic moment in Mary's life, when she knelt before her Lord, and cried, "Rabboni!" I gripped my Bible close to me with muscles tense and nerves vibrating. Under the inspiration of this vision, I wrote as quickly as the words could be formed, the poem exactly as it has since appeared. That same evening I wrote the music.

I experienced my own version of epiphany years ago. Easter morning in 1976 began beautifully. As I cooked breakfast, I turned on the radio to my favorite Christian station. The sermon by Dr. Ben Haden was entitled, "If a Man Die, Shall He Live Again?" I rejoiced as I listened to the words affirming my faith in eternal life.

The phone rang. I heard the news that my sister Margaret had died very suddenly. Shock, grief, and tears overwhelmed me. However, before I could get a flight to Virginia to be with Margaret's family, I went to church for the usual Easter celebration. I trembled in my weakness, but my faith was strong.

As I sat in the pew listening to the organ music, I glanced down at the bulletin in my lap. On the cover were two words: "He lives." Staring at those words, I was struck by another truth, and I penciled in the letter "S." The bulletin now read, "She Lives."

Death has been conquered for all believers, because Jesus lives. I knew that Margaret, too, was alive in heaven, just as I will be one day.

Lord, because your tomb was temporary, life with you is eternal. Hallelujah! Amen.

I come to the garden alone
while the dew is still on the roses,
and the voice I hear
falling on my ear,
the Son of God discloses.

Refrain: And he walks with me, and he talks with me,
and he tells me I am his own;
and the joy we share as we tarry there,
none other has ever known.

C. Austin Miles, 1913 (John 20:11-18)

23. It Is Well with My Soul

"May the God of peace himself sanctify you entirely; and may your spirit and soul and body be kept sound." (1 Thess. 5:23)

The Horatio Spafford family of Chicago planned an exciting vacation to Europe for the fall of 1873. When the time came, however, business matters in the Spafford law firm prevented Mr. Spafford from accompanying his family, but he expected to join them as soon as possible.

Anna Spafford and four of their daughters kissed him good-bye, then settled in on the beautiful French steamer *Ville du Havre* for the long journey. As the ship slipped out of port the children waved good-bye to their father for the last time.

Within a few days, on November 22, an English shipping vessel struck the hull of the ship carrying the Spaffords. It was cut apart and sank quickly. The girls were swept into the icy waters of the Atlantic with 222 other people, never to be found.

Their mother was rescued along with other survivors who were taken to Cardiff, Wales. There she wired her husband a brief but heart-wrenching message: "Saved alone." He left immediately to join his wife. As his ship neared the spot where the tragedy had occurred, the distraught father prayed. His words, written in the form of a poem, have since become the well-known hymn "It Is Well with My Soul." In Spafford's time of grief he spoke to his Lord, whom he had learned to love and trust in the past.

An earlier tragedy had come to the Spafford family; in 1871, the great Chicago fire had destroyed all of their possessions. Grief returned again when, in 1880, their only son, fourteen-year-old Horatio, died of scarlet fever.

Spafford's strong faith, revealed in these three verses of this beloved hymn, is a witness to the power of a loving God who can heal the brokenhearted. The soulful music that carries this prayer-hymn was composed by Philip Bliss, who was killed in a tragic accident a few days after its composition. He was only thirty-three years old.

Sadness and suffering can come so quickly. How will we get through it? We can seek love and understanding in godly people. If we are too weak to pray, we can ask them to pray for us. Together we will find strength in God's Word. That is the body of Christ in mission to one another.

Lord Jesus, I thank you for your provisions for our strength in weakness. In your name. Amen.

When peace, like a river, attendeth my way,
when sorrows like sea billows roll;
whatever my lot, thou hast taught me to say,
it is well, it is well with my soul.

Refrain: It is well with my soul,
it is well, it is well with my soul.

Horatio G. Spafford, 1873

24. JESUS LOVES ME

"As the Father has loved me, so I have loved you; abide in my love." (John 15:9)

This simple, childlike song has its beginnings in a very short poem in a very long novel. Today, millions of people know the poem "Jesus Loves Me." The novel has been forgotten. Anna Bartlett Warner wrote this poem for the book *Say and Seal,* which she coauthored with her sister Susan in 1860. One of the characters speaks the words of loving assurance to a dying child. "Jesus loves me, this I know, for the Bible tells me so."

The Warner sisters were born in New York State and lived all their lives along the Hudson River, adjacent to the West Point Military Academy. On Sunday mornings they taught Bible study classes to the cadets in their home.

When they died, each of the sisters was given military honors in recognition of their spiritual contributions to the cadets. Their home on Constitution Island was willed to the Academy and was made into a national shrine.

A well-known composer and publisher of gospel hymns,

William Bradbury, discovered this poem and developed it into the version we all know and love today. Feeling the simple power of its message, he added the chorus in 1861, which emphasizes its theme: "Yes, Jesus loves me! Yes, Jesus loves me! Yes, Jesus loves me! The Bible tells me so."

Karl Barth, one of the greatest theologians in this century, said that these first two lines capture the depths of the Christian gospel.

When I feel that what I do is not very significant, I remember the brevity of this little song and the millions of people it touches. The simple form can distract me from its deep, fundamental message. With God's love flowing through me, my simple deeds become mighty acts of God that produce abundant life.

Did I give a loving smile to a lonely person today? Did I pat a shoulder that is heavy with burdens? Did I give a cup of cold water to a thirsty soul?

Jesus, you bless me with your love and presence. Help me to reach out and love others in your name. Amen.

Jesus loves me! This I know,
for the Bible tells me so.
Little ones to him belong;
they are weak, but he is strong.

Refrain: Yes, Jesus loves me! Yes, Jesus loves me!
Yes, Jesus loves me! The Bible tells me so.

Anna B. Warner, 1860 (st. 1); David Rutherford McGuire (sts. 2-3)

25. Just As I Am, Without One Plea

"As Jesus was walking along, he saw a man . . . and he said to him, 'Follow me.' " (Matt. 9:9)

She could not believe the cold, hard facts. The prognosis of her disease was eventual paralysis. Born in Clapham, England, in 1789, Charlotte Elliott had experienced an active and normal life for thirty years, so the verdict about her future resulted in a very despondent and frustrated young woman. As the months grew into years, her frustrations grew into anger. Why would God allow such a thing to happen?

But one day, in 1822, a very special visitor came to the family home. The well-known Swiss evangelist, Caesar Malan, sat by her bedside. Seeking his wise counsel, Charlotte explained her hopelessness and despair. The question that got to the source of her anguish was "You speak of coming to Jesus, but how? I'm not fit to come."

Malan patiently explained the all-knowing, but all-forgiving and loving Savior. He told Charlotte that Jesus spoke of himself as the bread of life; that whoever comes to him will not hunger (John 6:35). As they prayed, she recognized her hungers. She wanted freedom from the depression that plagued her. She longed for peace and hope in her circumstances. It was a relief to say "Yes" to the simple request of Jesus: "Follow me."

The immediate change in her attitude was lasting. Each year she celebrated that day as the beginning of her new life— her spiritual birthday. On such a birthday in 1834, she captured her new insight on paper in the poem "Just As I Am." It expressed her "formula of faith" as she lovingly explained it to others. The music for her poem was later composed by American gospel musician William Bradbury.

For the remainder of her life, poetry was an expressive witness of her Christian faith. There were more than a hundred poems published in *The Invalid's Hymnbook*. Profits from its sales built a school for needy children. The director of the school, who was her brother and a minister, said: "In the course of my work, I hope to see some fruit of my ministry. But I feel more has been done by the single poem of my sister, 'Just As I Am.' "

Could it be that one little poem touched more lives than many sermons or a school for needy children? It would not seem possible. But multiplication can be a miracle in God's plan. After Charlotte's death at age eighty-two, more than a thousand letters were discovered in her papers from people around the world, expressing thankfulness that their lives had been redirected by this one hymn.

Precious Lamb of God, the call to follow you is exciting. You give more than this world could begin to offer. With my whole being, I come, I come. Amen.

Just as I am, without one plea,
but that thy blood was shed for me,
and that thou bidst me come to thee,
O Lamb of God, I come, I come!

Charlotte Elliott, 1835

26. MY JESUS, I LOVE THEE

"We love because he first loved us." (1 John 4:19)

The author's name was missing; only the name "Anonymous" appeared. But the poem was magnificent in its simplicity. Whoever wrote about such heartfelt commitment to Jesus must be an older Christian with years of experience in all facets of the faith.

These were the thoughts of composer and minister A. J. Gordon when he saw the hymn "My Jesus, I Love Thee" in *The London Hymn Book* (1864). He felt the tune was too weak to carry words of such depth, so he set about to compose the tune we sing today.

That's when it began a journey on wings of music that resulted in the discovery of its author, William Featherstone. Featherstone lived in Montreal, Canada, until his death in 1873 at the age of twenty-seven. The lasting impact of his life is in this prayer, written after his conversion while he was in his teens. To find the answer to life at such an early age is truly a blessing because growing up is difficult.

Having given birth to four children, I can imagine some of the emotions of William Featherstone. As I look more closely at the poem, I smile at the phrase "for thee all the follies of sin I resign." Imagine the follies of sin in the mid-1800s compared to the follies of sin in the twentieth century! But the root cause of sin—rebellion against God—never changes. Someone said this is the "me generation." If the first question is "What do I want?" the wrong choice can easily be made. Putting Jesus first is the only right choice.

This hymn reminds me that God first loved me. My love is a response. My pardon was purchased on Calvary's tree. Jesus wore those piercing thorns on his brow. How could my reponse be anything but love and commitment?

The last stanza is a picture of heaven. It is interesting that a young man who seemingly had a long life before him would have written so eloquently about the heavenly home. To delight in "mansions of glory" is from Jesus' words in John's Gospel: "In my Father's house are many mansions" (14:2*a*, KJV). To "sing with the glittering crown upon my brow" refers to the book of Revelation: "Around the throne are twenty-four thrones, and seated on the thrones are twenty-four elders, dressed in white robes, with golden crowns on their heads" (4:4).

These scripture verses fill me with joy. Glory awaits those who die in Christ.

My Jesus, I love you. I know you are mine for eternity. Amen.

My Jesus, I love thee, I know thou art mine;
for thee all the follies of sin I resign.
My gracious Redeemer, my Savior art thou;
if ever I loved thee, my Jesus, 'tis now.

William R. Featherstone, 1864

27. NEAR TO THE HEART OF GOD

"Draw near to God, and he will draw near to you."
(James 4:8)

In this noisy world of busy activity, it is a necessity to find time for quiet. I read in one of my favorite devotional books, *The Woman Within*, that Jan Meier feels the same:

"What happens when we find the time to be quiet and listen? God's wisdom looms larger and our problems shrink. Silence changes our perspective." Her words explain why it is essential to make the time to pull away from busy schedules and be still.

The beautiful hymn "Near to the Heart of God" speaks of those silent moments as a "quiet rest" and "comfort sweet." Cleland McAfee composed both words and music. Born in Ashley, Missouri, he later became a Presbyterian minister and was a dynamic preacher and teacher. During the years between 1912 and 1930 he was a professor of systematic theology at McCormick Seminary in Chicago.

But in the early part of his ministry, he pastored the campus church and directed the choir at Park College in Parkville, Missouri, where he had graduated in 1884. While there, he received word that two of his beloved nieces had died from diphtheria. The epidemic was sweeping over the entire nation at the turn of the century.

In his grief he turned to God's Word for strength, to God's promises for comfort. And he received an answer in the form of a song: "Near to the Heart of God." McAfee gathered the student choir in the yard of the little girls' family home and sang the comforting words. The following Sunday the hymn was sung at his church.

The descriptive words in the last stanza gave me inner peace and courage at the end of my mother's life. For months she lay in the bed of a nursing home, unable to get to that "place of full release, where all is joy and peace." Her heartbeat was very strong, so it seemed as if her pain would go on forever.

I knew she was ready to go to heaven and I was comforted by the powerful statement of faith in Psalm 73:24: "You will guide me with your counsel, and afterward you will take me into glory."

At her funeral on April 20, 1990, I told this story and sang "Near to the Heart of God." Tears of sadness ran down my cheeks, for I would miss her. But I was thankful for her full release from pain into her heavenly home.

"O Jesus, blest Redeemer, sent from the heart of God, hold us who wait before thee near to the heart of God." Amen.

There is a place of quiet rest,
near to the heart of God;
a place where sin cannot molest,
near to the heart of God.

Refrain: O Jesus, blest Redeemer, sent from the heart of God,
hold us who wait before thee near to the heart of God.

Cleland B. McAfee, 1903

28. NEARER, MY GOD, TO THEE

"I am with you and will keep you wherever you go." (Gen. 28:15)

The beautiful ship hit an iceberg on its maiden voyage. The rest of the story is well-documented history. The *Titanic* sank on April 15, 1912. Of the 2,227 people on board, more than 1,500 went to their deaths in the icy waters of the Atlantic. It has been said that the hymn "Nearer, My God to Thee" echoed through the night before the doomed ship finally sank beneath the waves.

Several years earlier some of these words were whispered from the lips of President William McKinley as he lay dying from an assassin's bullet: "Nearer my God to Thee . . . has been my constant prayer."

Both incidences show that in troubled times we long for the assurance of the ever-present strength of God.

Composer Sarah Flower Adams, born in 1805 in England, wrote the words that form the basis of the hymn. Her writing ability was joined with the musical talent of her sister, Eliza. Together they wrote several hymns, but "Nearer, My God, to Thee" is the one that is best remembered.

The words focus on the broken relationship in Genesis 28. Having tricked his father and stolen a precious gift from his brother Esau, Jacob fled into the desert. Lying down to sleep, Jacob had a dream. A ladder reached from earth to heaven.

On it were angels, and at the top he saw God, who assured Jacob of his presence. It was a beautiful prelude to Jacob and Esau's reconciliation years later.

God's promise was repeated to Joshua many years later, when he was chosen to lead the Israelites into the Promised Land after Moses died. "Be strong and of good courage; do not be afraid, nor be dismayed, for the LORD your God is with you wherever you go" (Josh. 1:9, NKJV).

The disciples heard the same promise hundreds of years later from Jesus, after he told them to go into all the world. "And lo, I am with you always, even to the end of the age" (Matt. 28:20, NKJV).

In times of desolation or tribulation, do not let fear control. God in all the power of the Holy Spirit is with us.

Dear God, the truth of your promise takes away all anxieties. Help us to draw nearer to you. In Jesus' name. Amen.

Nearer, my God, to thee, nearer to thee!
E'en though it be a cross that raiseth me,
still all my song shall be, nearer, my God, to thee;
nearer, my God to thee, nearer to thee!

Sarah F. Adams, 1841 (Gen. 28:10-22)

29. NOW THANK WE ALL OUR GOD

"Give thanks in all circumstances; for this is the will of God in Christ Jesus for you." (1 Thess. 5:18)

The natural response to someone who gives me a gift is to say "thank you." But if that person has done something that results in my resentment and hostility, "thank you" is difficult to express.

So it is with God's blessings. The natural response is praise and thanksgiving. But when circumstances in life are difficult, I often find myself in despair and ask, "Why me?" The biggest hindrance to my thankfulness seems to be my humanness.

That is not an uncommon dilemma. But when I study the background of "Now Thank We All Our God," I am astounded that the composer, Martin Rinkart, was living through years of bloodshed and suffering when he wrote these words.

A minister at the Lutheran church in Eilenburg, Germany, Rinkart faithfully served his people throughout the Thirty Years' War (1618–1648). Catholics and Protestants were in violent disagreement in the countries of central Europe and their battleground was Germany. Since Eilenburg was a city surrounded by walls, the refugee population grew rapidly. During the horrible plague of 1637 Rinkart had forty to fifty funerals a day. One funeral was that of his own wife.

Rinkart grieved with his people. But through his faith in God, who never fails to give love and strength, he continued to lead in worship and praise.

Later, when the Swedes were in control of the city, an unjust tax was imposed on the people. Pastor Rinkart's request to lower the taxes was to no avail. History records that he said to his congregation, "Come my children, we can find no mercy with man. Let us take refuge with God." So they knelt and prayed. The Swedish commander was so impressed with the confident Christians that he withdrew the high tax.

I can imagine the jubilant response of the people who were at the mercy of warring leaders. It must have happened exactly as the first words of this powerful hymn describe. With their "hearts, their hands and their voices," they were in awe of the wondrous things God was doing.

The second stanza becomes a prayer: "O may this bounteous God, through all our life be near us." A God who is always present is seen in Jesus, who said; "I am with you always, even to the end of the age" (Matt. 28:20, NKJV).

O God, I desire to be thankful always, regardless of my circumstances. Amen.

Now thank we all our God, with heart and hands and voices,
who wondrous things has done, in whom this world rejoices;
who, from our mothers' arms hath blessed us on our way
with countless gifts of love, and still is ours today.

Martin Rinkart, 1663; trans. by Catherine Winkworth, 1858

30. O For a Thousand Tongues to Sing

"Praise the LORD! How good it is to sing praises to our God; for he is gracious, and a song of praise is fitting." (Ps. 147:1)

The day Charles Wesley became aware of a fresh power of God, his life was never the same. He called it his conversion on May 21, 1738. The assurance of his salvation in Jesus Christ went from his head to his heart. Recorded in his journal on that Sunday are these words: "This is my day of Pentecost. I finally find myself at peace with God."

A year later he celebrated that memory as he wrote an anniversary hymn, "O For a Thousand Tongues to Sing." The idea was sparked by Wesley's spiritual mentor, Peter Böhler, who had joyfully remarked to Wesley, "Had I a thousand tongues, I would praise him with them all."

It is difficult to talk about Charles, who was born in 1707 in Epworth, England, and exclude his brother John, born four years earlier. The father of the large family of nineteen children was Samuel Wesley, an ordained priest in the Church of England. Their mother, Susanna, had a godly influence on her children as she diligently taught each one in the home.

Never could these parents have imagined the positive impact that their sons, John and Charles, would have on the decadent English society and the rigid liturgy of the Church. In May 1738, within three days of each other, John and Charles celebrated their "day of Pentecost." The power of the Holy Spirit flooded their souls. Praise was their natural response: John became a powerful preacher, while Charles became a prolific hymn writer.

Like Wesley, I finally found my peace with God when I had my day of Pentecost on September 1, 1979, in Paris, Tennessee. Even though I was a Christian, I did not fully understand what Jesus meant when he told his disciples, "John baptized with water, but in a few days you will be baptized with the Holy Spirit" (Acts 1:5, NIV). When I asked Jesus to fill me with the Holy Spirit, my faith gained a new dimension; it became a personal experience, not just a historical event.

Charles Wesley is a perfect example of a disciple before and after Pentecost. God's power assisted him "to proclaim and to spread through all the earth" the mighty name of Jesus.

Lord Jesus, your name is music in the ear, it is "life and health and peace." Bless your holy name. Amen.

O for a thousand tongues to sing
my great Redeemer's praise,
the glories of my God and King,
the triumphs of his grace!

Charles Wesley, 1739

31. O GOD OUR HELP IN AGES PAST

"Lord, you have been our dwelling place in all generations." (Ps. 90:1)

The seventeenth-century church was not known for its joyful music. It was somber and devoid of feeling. If words were sung that were not from the Bible, it was considered to be an insult to God.

One Sunday, young Isaac Watts complained of this to his father, who quickly replied, "Why don't you give us something better, young man!" It was a wise suggestion and history proves it was prophetic of his son's future.

That brief conversation set the stage for the development of Isaac Watts as a writer of hymns. He gave the world of Christendom more than six hundred songs of joyful worship within a lifetime of seventy-four years. One of his greatest works is "O God, Our Help in Ages Past," based on the words of Psalm 90.

Isaac Watts was born on July 17, 1674, in Southampton, England, the eldest of nine children in a Christian family where faith and courage were part of daily life. His father was often put in jail for his disagreement with some of the beliefs and practices in the Church of England. But temporary jail terms did not deter the family's involvement in the Congregational Church, which was, in fact, called a "Dissenting Church."

After college and ordination, Watts continued to be a

Dissenter when he accepted a call to become pastor at the Independent Congregation on Mark Lane in London. He dared to write and preach with new expressions of praise, emotion, and simplicity. But the intensity of his schedule of preaching, teaching, and book publishing led to failing health. When he died in 1748 he was buried in London's Bunhill Cemetery, the place reserved for Dissenting preachers.

But the Church of England recognized his contributions to Christianity. A monument was erected in his memory in 1779 in Westminster Abbey, where he is enshrined as "the father of English hymnody."

As we sing his paraphrases of the Psalms, the ancient words come alive. Rhyming words impress on our memory that in God "we dwell secure" and our "defense is sure."

Lord Jesus, today you are the same as you were yesterday, and the same as you will be tomorrow. You are our help, our hope, our shelter, our home for eternity. Thank you. Amen.

O God, our help in ages past,
our hope for years to come,
our shelter from the stormy blast,
and our eternal home!

Isaac Watts, 1719 (Ps. 90)

32. O Happy Day, That Fixed My Choice

"I have said these things to you so that my joy may be in you." (John 15:11*a*)

Not many people gave little Philip much hope. Born in London, England, in 1702, he was the youngest of twenty children. From birth he was plagued with illness. But as he went through school, it was evident that Philip Doddridge was destined for great things. He finished all schooling with honors and was offered a scholarship to Cambridge by the Duchess of

Bedford. The offer had a condition attached—that he would become an Anglican priest.

This gifted young man had his sights on another ministry, so he declined. Dissatisfied with the Church of England, he became a Dissenting minister. He served an independent church in Northampton for more than twenty years, stressing the need for evangelism. The leadership of Philip Doddridge was honored in 1736 when he was awarded a Doctor of Divinity degree from Aberdeen University.

His love for music was expressed in hymns that he used as sermon illustrations. He contributed to the revival of congregational singing in England. However, none were published until after his death. That unexpected death came in 1750, when he was only forty-eight years old. After a severe attack of tuberculosis, it was decided he must visit a warmer climate. With all intentions of returning to his beloved congregation, he set off for Portugal, but died en route.

Because of his many contributions to the spread of the gospel, all of England mourned his death. A friend published a collection of his hymns entitled: *Doddridge's Hymns, Founded on Various Texts in the Holy Scriptures.*

"O Happy Day" was one of those hymns. The Old Testament records that the southern kingdom of Judah rejoiced when they renewed their covenant with God: "[They] sought him with their whole desire, and he was found by them" (2 Chron. 15:15).

I heard this hymn for the first time in 1970. The contagious joy in the beautiful notes sung by Charles Middleton, a Junaluska Singer, still rings in my heart. I rejoice as I remember the day "that fixed my choice on thee, my Savior and my God."

O God, thank you for my "happy day" when Jesus came into my heart. Amen.

O happy day, that fixed my choice,
on thee, my Savior and my God!
Well may this glowing heart rejoice,
and tell its raptures all abroad.

Refrain: Happy day, happy day, when Jesus
washed my sins away!
He taught me how to watch and pray, and
live rejoicing every day.
Happy day, happy day, when Jesus washed my sins away!

Philip Doddridge, 1755; refrain from *The Wesleyan Sacred Harp*, 1854
(2 Chron. 15:15)

33. O JESUS, I HAVE PROMISED

"God is not unrighteous to forget your work and labour of
love." (Heb. 6:10*a*, KJV)

Some of my favorite hymns were written as a result of loving family relationships. Experiences within the family circle
are often a writer's inspiration. Fathers, mothers, sisters, and
brothers touch one another deeply with their words and
actions.

So it was with these loving words from a father to his
daughter and two sons on their confirmation day. He said, "I
have written a hymn containing all the important truths I
want you to remember when you are fully confirmed." John
Ernest Bode's concern for his children that Sunday in 1866
will never be forgotten. The "important truths" resulted in the
beloved hymn "O Jesus, I Have Promised."

The author was born in England in 1816. He was
ordained into the Anglican Church. In his faithful ministry he
was also a poet, professor, and musician. His hymns were published in *Hymns from the Gospel of the Day* (1860).

The original tune of "O Jesus, I Have Promised" is not
known. But in 1881, the familiar melody that we now sing was
printed with another hymn in *The Methodist Sunday School
Tune-Book* (London).

The more I sing this hymn, the more prayerful I become. I
pray with a sincere desire "to serve thee to the end" and not to
"wander from the pathway." The second stanza reminds me to
seek to feel God's presence near me because "the world is ever

near." I continue this prayer-hymn as I ask Jesus to "shield my soul from sin."

In the Gospels, Peter boldly proclaimed that even if all of the disciples fell away, he never would (Matt. 26:33). Peter did not keep his bold promise. Three times he denied knowing Jesus before the trial and Crucifixion. But the intentions of Peter's promise remained solid. He cried in humble repentance. After the Resurrection, the Lord asked him, "Do you love me?" Peter's quick reply was, "Lord, you know all things. You know that I love you" (John 21:17).

That is what gives me comfort as I sing these awesome promises. My Lord knows my failures. He knows when I stumble. He also knows my heart's desire to walk with him. In the last stanza, peace flows into my heart as I remember the promises of Jesus: where he is in glory, there I can be also.

Jesus, I have promised to follow you, my Master and my Friend. Amen.

O Jesus, I have promised to serve thee to the end;
be thou forever near me, my Master and my friend.
I shall not fear the battle if thou art by my side,
nor wander from the pathway if thou wilt be my guide.

John E. Bode, ca. 1866 (Luke 9:57)

34. O Little Town of Bethlehem

"But you, O Bethlehem of Ephrathah, who are one of the little clans of Judah, from you shall come forth for me one who is to rule in Israel." (Mic. 5:2)

Hearing about Bethlehem is not the same as being a part of it. Reading about the birth of Jesus is not the same as worshiping in the Church of the Nativity on Christmas Eve. These thoughts may well have been what went through

Phillips Brooks's mind after his visit to the Holy Land in 1865. When he returned to Philadelphia and his pastorate at Holy Trinity Church, the heartwarming memories never ceased.

Several years later when he wanted a new song of Christmas for the children to sing at church, he reached back for inspiration to his Holy Land visit. The poem he wrote in 1868 painted the sights and sounds of the wonderful little town he had visited. What came from his heart was a Christmas carol that has lived to become a worldwide favorite, "O Little Town of Bethlehem."

Brooks asked the church organist, Lewis Redner, to compose a simple melody for it. But nothing seemed to fit the mood of the melancholy words. One night, during a fretful sleep, Redner thought he heard music. Immediately he wrote the melody just as we sing it today. "I think it was a gift from heaven," Mr. Redner joyfully admitted.

Phillips Brooks was a beloved and respected evangelist. Born in Boston in 1825, and educated at Harvard, he became the bishop of the Boston area Episcopal churches. This giant of a man, who stood six feet, six inches tall, also had a big heart that endeared him to young and old alike. There were always toys in his office for any children who visited him. It was a familiar sight to see the beloved bishop sitting on the floor playing a game with a group of children. He never married, but other people's children became family to him. When he died unexpectedly at age fifty-eight, his extended family was overwhelmed with grief.

A child put his death in perspective. When told by her mother that Bishop Brooks had gone to heaven, the little girl simply replied, "Oh Mama, how happy the angels will be!"

Our Lord Emmanuel, thank you for coming to us and abiding with us. Amen.

O little town of Bethlehem, how still we see thee lie;
above thy deep and dreamless sleep the silent stars go by.
Yet in thy dark streets shineth the everlasting light;
the hopes and fears of all the years are met in thee tonight.

Phillips Brooks, ca. 1868

35. O Love That Will Not Let Me Go

"There is no fear in love, but perfect love casts out fear."
(1 John 4:18a)

Love. This magnificent four-letter word holds us in its power. Everyone longs to be loved. The lack of it leads to heartache and despair. This seems to have been the reason for the writing of the poem "O Love That Will Not Let Me Go." The author, George Matheson, was a Presbyterian minister who had lost his eyesight. Some believe he lost the woman he planned to marry because she feared a future with a blind husband.

It will never be known for certain, for Matheson's own words did not reveal the reason for his heartache. In his journal entry of June 6, 1882, he wrote:

> I was alone in the manse. . . . the night of my sister's marriage. Something happened to me which is known only to myself, and which caused me the most severe mental suffering. The hymn was the fruit of that suffering. It was the quickest bit of work I ever did in my life. . . . the whole work was completed in five minutes.

The following year Albert Peace, an organist and music editor of *The Scottish Hymnal,* composed the music for this inspiring poem. He described it this way: "After reading the poem carefully, I wrote the music straight off, and must say that the ink of the first note was hardly dry when I had finished the tune."

George Matheson was born in Glasgow, Scotland, on March 27, 1842. He had only partial sight from birth and his eyes grew weaker until he was totally blind at age eighteen. His academic progress was not hindered, however: he later graduated with honors from the University of Edinburgh.

Throughout his ministry, the coworker who helped with sermon memorization and pastoral duties was his devoted sister. He pastored the two-thousand-member St. Bernard's Parish Church in Edinburgh for the last years of his ministry. He died in 1906 at the age of sixty-four—one of Scotland's most eloquent preachers.

The "severe mental suffering" experienced by George Matheson inspired him to write a hymn that speaks to the deep longing for love. The sustaining love of God is perfectly described in each of the verses: "O Love," "O Light," "O Joy," "O Cross." We find eternal hope and comfort in any circumstance.

Dear God, thank you for your never-changing love that allows me to "trace the rainbow through the rain." In Jesus' name. Amen.

O Love that will not let me go,
I rest my weary soul in thee;
I give thee back the life I owe,
that in thine ocean depths its flow
may richer, fuller be.

George Matheson, 1882

36. O PERFECT LOVE

"A man will leave his father and mother and be united to his wife, and they will become one flesh." (Gen. 2:24, NIV)

Excitement was growing as the family made plans for the upcoming wedding. But it was difficult to find just the right music. The hymn that was written for this special occasion in 1883 was "O Perfect Love." The bride's sister, Dorothy B. Gurney, explains why she wrote it:

We were all singing hymns one Sunday evening and had just finished "Strength and Stay," a special favorite of my sister, when someone remarked what a pity it was that the words should be unsuitable for a wedding. My sister, turning suddenly to me, said: "What is the use of a sister who composes poetry, if she cannot write me new words to this tune. "

Dorothy agreed to try to compose such a poem and went into the library. After fifteen minutes she returned with text in hand. They sang the favorite hymn tune again, but this time with the words Dorothy had just written, a poem entitled "O Perfect Love." The words and tune blended; the new song was joyfully received and sung at the wedding.

The popularity of this prayer-hymn for weddings in London was instant. Soon it was published for wider distribution. After a decade, it was incorporated into a fuller anthem for the wedding ceremony of the Duke and Duchess of Fife.

Writing was a natural gift for Dorothy Gurney. Born in London, England, in 1858, she was nurtured in the faith of her Anglican grandfather and father. She expressed that faith in her poetry. Several volumes were published while she was still young. One of the most famous quotations from a poem she wrote is, "One is nearer God's heart in a garden than anywhere else on earth."

Of all the words that flowed from the heart and soul of this composer, none are so wonderful to me as "O Perfect Love." The thrill of my wedding day is fresh each time I hear it. It is a perfect prayer to the One who is perfect Love. Our Lord is the example of self-giving, understanding love. We continue to pray for the "patient hope and quiet, brave endurance" in stanza 2, because every marriage has its difficulties. God hears our prayers and "grants us the peace which calms all earthly strife."

O perfect Life, thank you for your perfect Love that gives strength and guidance. Amen.

O perfect Love, all human thought transcending,
lowly we kneel in prayer before thy throne,
that theirs may be the love which knows no ending,
whom thou forevermore dost join in one.

Dorothy B. Gurney, 1883

37. ONWARD CHRISTIAN SOLDIERS

"Endure hardship with us like a good soldier of Christ Jesus." (2 Tim. 2:3, NIV)

Music written for children usually stays within that age group. But not so with this rousing song that has traveled to many lands and is sung by people of all ages. "Onward, Christian Soldiers" was written in 1864 by Sabine Baring-Gould, an English clergyman. He said it was written for a day of school festivals in Yorkshire:

> It was arranged that our school should join its forces with that of a neighboring village. I wanted the children to sing when marching from one village to the other, but couldn't think of anything quite suitable, so I sat up at night resolved to write something myself. "Onward, Christian Soldiers" was the result. It was written in great haste, likely in less than 15 minutes.

Baring-Gould was one of the most versatile writers of the nineteenth century. He wrote more than eighty-five books on various subjects, but this hymn, which was not intended for publication, is his best-known work. The joyful music was composed by Arthur S. Sullivan.

I imagine a festive group of children marching through the streets behind the cross of Jesus. The qualities of a child's faith remind me that Jesus said, "Whoever does not receive the kingdom of God as a little child will never enter it" (Mark 10:15).

Hymnist Evelyn Bence says, "We do well to teach and show our children that the Christian faith is full of paradox. Yes, we are sheep safely grazing under the watchful eye of the Good Shepherd. At the same time we are called to choose whom we will serve; we are to bear witness to our allegiance to the King of Kings."

This is a mysterious combination that I did not understand for a long time into my faith journey. The loving and peaceful relationship with Jesus is to be combined with his marching orders, which direct me outward into witness. Without that essential element the early church in the book of Acts would have lain dormant.

So I am learning not to be ashamed of the gospel of Jesus Christ. Let's sing it, preach it, shout it, and always be ready to share it with others. An annual March for Jesus began in the 1980s in England. The idea rapidly spread throughout the world. Millions of joyful Christians from many denominations gather in May to march through the streets of their city behind the cross of Jesus. They sing the same "good news" that was sung by a small group of school children who marched through their village in England over a century ago.

O Jesus, infiltrate my being so I can make your footprints on this world. Amen.

Onward, Christian soldiers, marching as to war,
with the cross of Jesus going on before.
Christ, the royal Master, leads against the foe;
forward into battle see his banners go!

Refrain: Onward, Christian soldiers, marching as to war,
with the cross of Jesus going on before.

Sabine Baring-Gould, 1864

38. ROCK OF AGES, CLEFT FOR ME

"Trust in the LORD forever, for the LORD, the LORD, is the Rock eternal." (Isa. 26:4, NIV)

A hymn can be born out of grief, joy, or a search for deeper meaning in life. But the magnificent hymn "Rock of Ages" was born out of very different circumstances. Its author, Augustus Toplady, was born in Farnham, England, in 1740 and began school in London. He then attended Trinity College in Dublin, Ireland. While there he experienced a dramatic conversion at the age of sixteen. Toplady wrote this account:

> Strange that I, who had so long sat under the means of grace in England, should be brought right with God in an obscure part of Ireland, in a barn by the ministry of one who could hardly spell his name. Surely it was the Lord's doing and it is marvelous.

After graduation he returned to England, where he was ordained for ministry in the Anglican Church. He was acquainted with John Wesley, but their theological differences brought conflict into their relationship. Toplady believed the teaching of John Calvin: some are chosen or predestined to accept the Lord. This was in opposition to Wesley's Arminian view that each person has a free will to choose or reject salvation.

In 1776 Toplady, who was the editor of *The Gospel Magazine,* wrote about the bitter controversy. His poem "Rock of Ages" concluded the article, using phrases that spoke of his strong convictions.

Author Kenneth W. Osbeck, in writing about this hymn, focuses our attention on the positive view of the controversy: "Despite the belligerent intent of this text, God has preserved this hymn for more than 200 years to bring blessing to both Arminian and Calvinistic believers around the world."

Augustus Toplady was known and respected as a zealous evangelical preacher. He died from tuberculosis in 1778 at the age of thirty-eight. Continuing to proclaim his faith, some of his last words were: "My heart beats every day stronger and stronger for glory. Sickness is no affliction. . . . My prayers are now all converted to praise."

More than a century later, an amazing woman, Corrie ten Boom, survived the horrors of a Nazi concentration camp because of her faith. She knew that Jesus was her Rock. He was her "hiding place from the wind, a cover from the tempest . . . the shadow of a great rock in a weary land" (Isa. 32:2, NKJV). The Rock of all ages is present for all believers.

Lord, lead me on, help me stand in the shelter of your loving protection. Amen.

Rock of Ages, cleft for me,
let me hide myself in thee;
let the water and the blood,
from thy wounded side which flowed,
be of sin the double cure;
save from wrath and make me pure.

Augustus M. Toplady, 1776

39. Silent Night, Holy Night

" 'Look, the virgin shall conceive and bear a son, and they shall name him Emmanuel,' which means, 'God is with us.' " (Matt. 1:23)

Joseph Mohr, the priest at St. Nicholas's Church in Oberndorf, Austria, hurriedly wrote the words to this song for the Christmas Eve service. Otherwise there would have been no music because the organ was broken. He asked his friend Franz Gruber to compose a tune for the poem. So on December 24, 1818, the two friends sang it together, with Gruber accompanying on his guitar. It was simple. It was gorgeous.

From a tiny village that night an unknown Christmas carol began its worldwide journey. When an organ repairman came to the church a few days later, he discovered the song jotted down on a piece of paper. Asking if he could share it with others, it eventually got into the hands of a well-known singing family, who included it in their concerts. It arrived in America with the German-speaking immigrants; the first publication in English was in 1849 in a Methodist hymnal.

Music about the birth of Jesus reminds us of the angels who sang to announce that moment in history. As we get closer to the celebration of that event each year, it is still exciting to hear the familiar carols. After the holidays are over, I often feel melancholy as the carols fade away, not to be sung again until the next year.

A child asked a very important question one day. She and her mother were putting away the Christmas decorations. When they had carefully wrapped the manger scene, boxed and stored it in the hall closet, little Mandy asked: "Will Jesus be back next year?"

"Oh, yes, Mandy," her mother replied. "In fact, he is never gone, but is alive and never leaves us." She quickly described the difference between the lovely ceramic figure and the Baby who lives all year. It was a perfect time to pray with Mandy and thank God for the real Jesus.

Lord Jesus, thank you for silent and holy times to remember your birth into the world and our hearts. Amen.

Silent night, holy night,
all is calm, all is bright
round yon virgin mother and child.
Holy infant, so tender and mild,
sleep in heavenly peace,
sleep in heavenly peace.

Joseph Mohr, 1818, alt.; sts. 1, 2, 3 trans. by John F. Young;
st. 4 trans. anon. (Luke 2:6-20)

40. SOFTLY AND TENDERLY JESUS IS CALLING

"I therefore, the prisoner in the Lord, beg you to lead a life worthy of the calling to which you have been called." (Eph. 4:1)

The dynamic preaching of evangelist Dwight L. Moody was over: he lay on his deathbed. Composer Will Thompson sat by that bed for their final visit. Dr. Moody gestured to his friend. Thompson leaned in close.

"Will," said Moody, "I had rather have written 'Softly and Tenderly' than anything I have been able to do in my life."

Will Thompson, author of "Softly and Tenderly," was born on November 7, 1849, in Beaver County, Pennsylvania, but the family soon moved to East Liverpool, Ohio. His father, who was a banker and member of the Ohio state legislature, urged his son to enter the business world.

But music was an integral part of Will's makeup. He enrolled instead at the New England Conservatory of Music and graduated with honors. When he established his own publishing firm in his hometown, the business prospered, as did his talent for composing and singing. At that time, his interest centered on patriotic and popular songs.

But one day, as he sat in one of Dwight Moody's evangelistic crusades, Thompson was mightily touched by the hand of God. He experienced a major change in his outlook on life. He now wanted to write songs that would lead others to a deeper knowledge of God's revelation in Jesus Christ. He had a new mission: "Softly and Tenderly" became a symbol of that new vision.

Although we do not know the exact circumstances of the song's birth in 1880, the line "Ye who are weary, come home," is very revealing. Could it be that Will Thompson remembered his earlier resistance to God's call?

That phrase also reminds me of Jesus' call in Matthew 11:28: "Come to me, all you that are weary and are carrying heavy burdens, and I will give you rest." Even though I have answered God's call to discipleship, I get weary. When I wrestle with decisions that are confusing, I must listen to the soft and tender call of Jesus and ask for his direction.

The final call that comes to everyone is death. I am at peace when I read the promise of Jesus in John 14:2, "In my father's house are many mansions. . . . I go to prepare a place for you" (KJV).

Lord, keep the ear of my heart open to your voice. Amen.

Softly and tenderly Jesus is calling,
calling for you and for me;
see, on the portals he's waiting and watching,
watching for you and for me.

Refrain: Come home, come home; you who
are weary, come home;
earnestly, tenderly, Jesus is calling, calling,
O sinner, come home!

Will L. Thompson, 1880

41. STAND UP, STAND UP FOR JESUS

"Take up the whole armor of God, so that you may be able to withstand on that evil day, and having done everything, to stand firm." (Eph. 6:13)

Revival swept through the town of Philadelphia in 1858. All churches were being filled with people who were hungry to find deeper meaning in their lives. But one day tragedy struck, and the whole town mourned the death of a young and dynamic minister, Dudley Tyng. The accident at his home caused the loss of his arm. Profuse bleeding and an infection led to his death. But before he died, he whispered to his close friend, Rev. George Duffield, "Tell them, let us all stand up for Jesus."

The following Sunday, Duffield's sermon was based on the text from Ephesians 6:14: "Stand therefore, and fasten the belt of truth around your waist, and put on the breastplate of righteousness." It was preached in memory of his friend. When he finished the sermon, he read a poem he had written, "Stand Up, Stand Up for Jesus."

It is the event most remembered in Rev. Duffield's long ministry. Ordained a Presbyterian minister in 1840, he served churches in six different states. He died in 1888 at the home of his son, Samuel, who was the fourth-generation Presbyterian minister in the family.

"Stand Up, Stand Up for Jesus" reminds us that to be aware of our spiritual battles with evil in the world is the first step toward victory. The hymn gives hope from its beginning: "From victory unto victory his army shall he lead, till every foe is vanquished, and Christ is Lord indeed."

The courage of an Amish woman in Ethridge, Tennessee, was reported in *The Tennessean* newspaper. A tornado ripped through the small community one afternoon in April 1998. The woman survived even though she had no shelter. When someone peeked out the door of a grocery store seconds afterward, they saw her and asked where she hid when the tornado struck.

"I didn't," she said. "I just stood here and hugged my horse so it wouldn't be scared." Such bravery and faith are an inspiration to all of us who face life's "tornadoes."

O Jesus, I long to stand up in your strength. Through any danger, thank you for your presence. Amen.

Stand up, stand up for Jesus,
ye soldiers of the cross:
lift high his royal banner,
it must not suffer loss.

From victory unto victory
his army shall he lead,
till every foe is vanquished,
and Christ is Lord indeed.

George Duffield, Jr., 1858 (Eph. 6:10-17)

42. STANDING ON THE PROMISES

"For no matter how many promises God has made, they are 'Yes,' in Christ." (2 Cor. 1:20*a*, NIV)

Every employer wants to have workers who will do honest work and keep their promises. We all want those kinds of friends. However, no person can be perfect and every relationship has its moments of disappointments.

Where is the perfect promise from the perfect Person? Russell Kelso Carter gave us this answer in 1886, in this rousing hymn of assurance, "Standing on the Promises." Carter was born in Baltimore, Maryland, in 1849, and possessed a deep faith in the promises of God. He felt "bound to him eternally by love's strong cord." The promises "cannot fail" even when the "howling storms of doubt assail."

The music has a strong military cadence, a reminder that its author graduated from the Pennsylvania Military Academy and later became a professor there. He published textbooks, hymnbooks, and novels; he was also a minister and a physician. His life was full with various forms of service. Carter repeatedly returned to the secure promises of God.

In the opening phrase of this hymn, Carter wrote of his relationship with Christ: "Glory in the highest, I will shout and sing, standing on the promises of God." In John 3:16 we find one of the richest promises in the Bible. God loves us and sent Jesus to save us so that we would not perish but have everlasting life.

When we stand on that promise, we ask Jesus to be our Lord and Savior, and to have a life that has meaning and purpose. Then we understand his promise, "I came that they may have life, and have it abundantly" (John 10:10).

Oswald Chambers also focuses on that abundant life: "We must never measure our spiritual capacity on the basis of our education or our intellect; ... it is measured on the basis of the promises of God."

Lord God, I stand on your promises and joyfully receive abundant, eternal life. In Jesus' name. Amen.

Standing on the promises of Christ my King,
through eternal ages let his praises ring;
glory in the highest, I will shout and sing,
standing on the promises of God.

Refrain: Standing, standing, standing on the promises
of God my Savior;
standing, standing, I'm standing on the
promises of God.

R. Kelso Carter, 1886 (Eph. 6:14-17)

43. Sweet Hour of Prayer

"Call to me and I will answer you, and will tell you great and hidden things that you have not known." (Jer. 33:3)

It is a mystery. Who was William Walford? Some believe he was a blind shopkeeper in the village of Coleshill, Warwickshire, England, who asked a friend to write down a poem that was forming in his mind. Others believe he was a clergyman in that town who gave a copy of this poem to his friend and fellow clergyman, Thomas Salmon.

We will probably never know for sure. But it is a fact that a Rev. Thomas Salmon, a minister in a Warwickshire church in 1842, received a special poem entitled "Sweet Hour of Prayer" from its author, William Walford, whose Christian commitment is revealed in the words. When Salmon returned to America following his pastorate in England, he sent the poem to the publisher of the *New York Observer*. It was printed in the September 1845 edition of the newspaper.

Musician William B. Bradbury was touched by its simple but profound message. He composed a beautiful melody that became the wings for carrying the message out into the world. The identity of poet William Walford remains a mystery, but so is prayer. As I read the disciples' request to Jesus, "Lord, teach us to pray" (Luke 11:1*b*), I recognize my own need to be taught.

Years ago, my whole life was changed when I realized that I did not know how to pray. I was alone in the waiting room of a hospital in New Mexico. Fear enveloped me as I waited while my nine-year-old son had emergency surgery.

I picked up a magazine called *Adventures in Prayer*. The author, Catherine Marshall, described her experiences in prayer, which did not resemble anything I knew. She prayed as if she were actually talking to God as a real person. That relationship sounded too good to be true, but I longed to experience it. I knew that all of my church attendance since childhood, marrying a minister, and becoming a missionary would not sustain me during those anxious moments.

So I began to pray. "Lord, are you listening? I have never known you. But I want to. Help me." I could not imagine what would happen. This was the most exciting prayer I had ever uttered. I believed and I waited. Soon I began to experience the awesome presence of God that never ceases. The words in the last stanza of "Sweet Hour of Prayer" say exactly what I know to be true: "Since he bids me seek his face, believe his word and trust his grace, I'll cast on him my every care."

Lord God, thank you for that desire to discover that you are real and for the opportunity to talk with you. Amen.

Sweet hour of prayer! sweet hour of prayer! that calls me
from a world of care,
and bids me at my Father's throne make all my
wants and wishes known.
In seasons of distress and grief, my soul has often found relief,
and oft escaped the tempter's snare by thy return,
sweet hour of prayer!

William Walford, 1845

44. Tell Me the Stories of Jesus

"Keep these words that I am commanding you today in
your heart. Recite them to your children and talk about them."
(Deut. 6:6a)

The Sunday school class was almost over and the children were restless. Their teacher, Mr. William Parker, put
away all the materials and began to tell them a story. It
worked every time. Quickly they became quiet and attentive.

Later that afternoon after church, Parker thought about
the countless times his students had said, "Please tell us another story." Suddenly an idea flashed into his mind, and he gathered his thoughts and arranged them in a poem: "Tell me the
stories of Jesus."

With those first words as a beginning, he continued to
write with vivid description about many events in Jesus' life.
The verses explain what it must have felt like to be blessed at
his knee, to sing glad hosannas while waving palm branches,
and to stand at the cross of bitter pain.

William H. Parker was born in Nottinghamshire, England,
on March 4, 1845, and died there in 1929. He worked for an
insurance company and was a dedicated Christian layman in
his home church, Chelsea Street Baptist. A friend described
him as a person who was "quiet in demeanor, kindly in dispo-
sition, always trying to see the best in others. He was one of
God's true gentlemen, respected and loved by all."

Parker's poem, "Tell Me the Stories of Jesus," was written
to honor the devotion of the pupils he taught each Sunday. It
was not used as a hymn for several years because it had no
music. The beautiful melody, written by Frederick A.
Challinor, was chosen as a result of a competition held by the
Sunday School Union of the Church of England in 1903.

"Tell Me the Stories of Jesus" is dear to me because
Sunday school thoughts flood my memory whenever I hear it.
My teacher, Jane McDonald, was a petite woman who had a
light of happiness on her face when she told us stories of Jesus.
Reading them in the Bible was not as exciting as when she told
them. She wanted us to feel what the people felt when they
were with Jesus.

Jesus told his disciples that the children who eagerly came
to him were an example for all: "Whoever does not receive the

kingdom of God as a little child will never enter it" (Mark 10:15).

Jesus my Lord, I am thankful I heard about you as a child. Now I know you in a deeper way, but I still must come as a little child with love and trust. Amen.

Tell me the stories of Jesus I love to hear;
things I would ask him to tell me if he were here:
scenes by the wayside, tales of the sea,
stories of Jesus, tell them to me.

William H. Parker, 1885 (Matt. 19:13-15; 21:8-9)

45. THERE'S WITHIN MY HEART A MELODY

"How could we sing the LORD's song in a foreign land?" (Ps. 137:4)

The news was devastating. It came to Luther Bridgers when he was preaching a revival in 1910 in Kentucky. His wife and three sons had stayed in Harrodsburg with her parents while he was away. But fire destroyed the home and his family perished.

When the young husband and father returned to Harrodsburg, he experienced grief he had never known before. His soul traveled into new territory—a dark valley of sorrow. How could he sing a song of faith with a broken heart—his "foreign land"?

Bridgers stood strong in his faith as he went to the Word of God. The Psalms were comforting because every human emotion is found there. The question in Psalm 137:4 echoed his own despair. The Israelites wept when they were forced from their homes into exile: "On the day I called, you answered me, you increased my strength of soul" (Ps. 138:3). Their hope was renewed.

So it was for Luther Bridgers. The process of healing began. Soon a song was born in which he expressed his bedrock faith. He was inspired to write the words and music for "There's Within My Heart a Melody." The melody seems to come from the "sweet and low whisper" of Jesus, who says: "Fear not, I am with thee, peace be still, in all of life's ebb and flow." Life has the ebb and flow of trials, but "though sometimes the path seems rough and steep, see his footprints all the way."

I have seen the footprints of Jesus in the life of one who has been touched by deep sorrow. My friend Glenda knows the God who comforts, sustains, and heals the brokenhearted. When her husband, Paul Ray Troutt, was serving a church in Lawrenceburg, Tennessee, a terrible tragedy occurred. On a hot August day in 1971, their car was hit by a drunk driver. Paul Ray and their two young sons were killed instantly. Glenda received severe injuries but she slowly recovered.

In the past years she has been a part of Mothers Against Drunk Driving. In a recent letter she wrote; "I feel that God has been able to use the tragedy of my life to bring comfort to others who are experiencing the same devastation."

Is my faith growing so that, if such a tragedy comes into my life, I am sustained in my grief? Will I hear the melody of God's love?

Lord, you are with me, and that is my security. Amen.

There's within my heart a melody
Jesus whispers sweet and low:
Fear not, I am with thee, peace be still,
in all of life's ebb and flow.

Refrain: Jesus, Jesus, Jesus, sweetest name I know,
fills my every longing, keeps me singing as I go.

Luther B. Bridgers, 1910

46. TO GOD BE THE GLORY

"But God forbid that I should glory, save in the cross of our Lord Jesus Christ." (Gal. 6:14*a*, KJV)

Among the thousands of hymns written by Fanny Crosby, this is one of the "brightest and best." In fact, that is the name of the songbook compiled in 1875 in which it first appeared. Composer William H. Doane, a friend and coworker, often wrote melodies for the words that the prolific poet compiled.

In the early days of Fanny Crosby's life, this little blind girl was taught the faith by her grandmother. Her blindness did not hinder her, for she memorized anything that was read to her. At a young age she could recite the first five books of the Bible and the four Gospels. Expressing her faith through poetry was a gift of genius.

Born Frances Jane, "Fanny" came into the world on March 24, 1820, in Putnam County, New York. Her quick mind and cheerful attitude made her a joy for all to know. She attended the New York School for the Blind, where she remained as a teacher for many years. In addition to teaching, she ministered to the poor in the slums of New York, and she wrote the words to more than eight thousand hymns during her ninety-five years.

"To God Be the Glory" lay quietly awaiting its debut for decades. Maybe it was set aside while the more typical Fanny Crosby hymns reached the masses. Whatever the reason, it was unpublished until the 1950s, when Cliff Barrows introduced it to the world during a Billy Graham Crusade in England. It appeared to be a new hymn, but it was an old hymn given a second birth. Since then, thousands of joyful voices have captured its majesty.

Speaking and singing praise to God is strengthening to the soul. But what happens when I don't feel like it? Does discouragement and discord draw me away from praise? I have discovered that a surprising joy "floods my soul" when I praise God, even if it is just out of obedience to his word that I do so. "And the Word became flesh and lived among us, and we have seen his glory . . . full of grace and truth" (John 1:14). That is sufficient reason to praise God.

Lord Jesus, I see your glory. It never fades, but I fail. Keep me faithful to praise in all circumstances. Amen.

To God be the glory, great things he hath done!
So loved he the world that he gave us his Son,
who yielded his life an atonement for sin,
and opened the lifegate that all may go in.

Refrain: Praise the Lord, praise the Lord, let the
earth hear his voice!
Praise the Lord, praise the Lord, let the people rejoice!
O come to the Father through Jesus the Son,
and give him the glory, great things he hath done!

Fanny J. Crosby, 1875

47. TRUST AND OBEY

"Those who love me will keep my word." (John 14:23*a*)

One night in Brockton, Massachusetts, over a century ago,
several key ingredients came together to give birth to a favorite
hymn, "Trust and Obey." A series of meetings were in progress
with evangelist D. L. Moody. During the "testimony time" a
young man rose to his feet and said, "I am not quite sure—but I
am going to trust, and I am going to obey." The statement
caught the attention of song leader Daniel B. Towner.

Jotting the sentence down, Towner mailed it, with the story
of its origin, to his friend Rev. J. H. Sammis, asking if he could
write a hymn to complete the thought. Sammis responded with
the words for the chorus, which captures the theme of the four
verses: "Trust and obey, for there's no other way to be happy in
Jesus." Towner then composed the music. With a sequence of
only six notes, he completed a hymn that has gone all over the
world in many languages. It was published that same year
(1887) in *Hymns Old and New*.

Daniel B. Towner was born into a musical family in 1850 in
Rome, Pennsylvania. His father was his first music teacher.
After formal training, he was music director for Methodist
churches in different states. He was then appointed the first

director of music at the Moody Bible Institute in Chicago. He died in 1919 while leading singing at a revival.

J. H. Sammis was born in Brooklyn, New York, in 1856. He entered the business world and was on staff at the YMCA when he felt God's call to preach. After finishing theological training, he was ordained to the Presbyterian ministry in 1880, where he served faithfully until his death.

Who was the young man who testified that he would trust and obey? Only God knows his name and whether he was able to keep his promise. But what he said that night in 1877 has led thousands of people to contemplate their own desire to trust and obey.

In his book, *The Wounded Heart*, Dan Allender says: "The biblical path allows for choice and responsible action but it involves walking through the valley without lighting a flaming torch in the darkness. Trusting in God involves the loss of our agenda . . . in humble dependence on God and passionate involvement with others."

In the last stanza of this hymn we focus on the future, which is unknown but secure if we believe "what he says we will do, where he sends we will go, never fear, only trust and obey." Uncertainty becomes certainty when Jesus is in control.

Lord, I want to trust in your Word and obey your guidance. Amen.

When we walk with the Lord in the light of his word,
what a glory he sheds on our way! While we do his good will,
he abides with us still, and with all who will trust and obey.

Refrain: Trust and obey, for there's no other way
to be happy in Jesus, but to trust and obey.

John H. Sammis, 1887 (1 John 1:7)

48. WE THREE KINGS

"They offered him gifts of gold, frankincense, and myrrh."
(Matt. 2:11*b*)

Thousands of children have portrayed the wise men who brought gifts to the Christ Child at his birth. The story is derived from Matthew 2:1-12, which is the only biblical reference to this event. It is beautifully captured in the majestic hymn "We Three Kings." Although there is no specific number of kings mentioned, it is assumed that each gift was carried by one man.

The number involved is not essential for this Christmas message. The gifts are symbols that explain the purpose of Jesus' coming. In stanza 2, "gold I bring to crown him again" signifies that Jesus is the King. Stanza 3 speaks of the gift of frankincense, which is the incense that denotes prayer and praise in Jesus' priestly ministry. In stanza 4, the gift of myrrh and "its bitter perfume breathes a life of gathering gloom," points to Jesus' suffering in death.

John Henry Hopkins composed the words and music in 1857. His intent to lift up this great event of praise and worship was eagerly received by his congregation and continues to add beauty to the Christmas season.

Hopkins was born in Pennsylvania in 1820. As a minister ordained in the Episcopal church, he was also a leader in the development of hymnody in that denomination. He was the first instructor in church music at General Theological Seminary in New York City. His popular publication, *Carols, Hymns and Songs* was reprinted four times. "We Three Kings" is the most well-known song from that collection.

After the first stanza, the words move from the activity of the three kings to a personal involvement. The personal pronoun "I" is used in the remainder of the carol. Do I bring him gold, frankincense, or myrrh? Do I offer him "prayer and praising, voices raising, worshiping God on high"?

The message is clear: I am responsible for my gifts to Jesus. I chose to give my heart years ago. Each morning when I awake, that continues to be my choice.

Lord Jesus, like the wise kings of long ago, help me to give Christmas gifts that reflect my love for you. Amen.

We three kings of Orient are;
bearing gifts we traverse afar,
field and fountain,
moor and mountain,
following yonder star.

Refrain: O star of wonder, star of light, star with
royal beauty bright,
westward leading, still proceeding, guide us to
thy perfect light.

John H. Hopkins, Jr., 1857 (Matt. 2:1-12)

49. Were You There

"But they shouted all the more, 'Crucify him!' " (Mark 15:14*b*)

When I was a child our family had a housekeeper. Lurline Argo was a blessing to my life. Before I knew there was racial prejudice, I loved this woman whose skin was much darker than mine. She loved me, too, and was one of the foundations of my childhood. One morning I heard her singing in the kitchen. The plaintive notes of "Were You There" drew me to her side. I could feel the love and reverence with which she sang, even though I was too young to understand the depth of the message.

Now I know the message and the Person it is about. The Gospel accounts of the Crucifixion of Jesus never cease to make me sorrowful. I feel the intensity of the song when I sing: "Sometimes it causes me to tremble, tremble, tremble."

Within all the spirituals is a blend of African heritage and memories of slave days in the United States. The essential element, however, is the heartfelt interpretation of biblical stories and the commitment to Jesus as Lord. Even though there was bondage in slavery here on earth, there was freedom in him. There was joy in knowing the beloved Savior. So it was natural to want to learn and sing about every detail of his life.

Before the assistance of the printed page, it was necessary to teach all folk music with repetitious phrases. So as we sing this hymn we repeat the same question over and over again, "Were you there when . . . ?" Even though I wasn't with Jesus to watch as he was "nailed to the tree" or "pierced in the side" or "laid in the tomb," I feel deeply involved in the event of suffering and tears.

Millions of people heard the music and the message of the spirituals in the late 1800s from the Fisk Jubilee Singers. They were students who formed a musical group on the campus of Fisk University in Nashville, Tennessee. The group became famous as they traveled abroad, singing their faith through the soul-stirring spirituals.

We learn the origin of many spirituals in *New Jubilee Songs* (1901) and *Folk Songs of the American Negro* (1907), two books that were published through the efforts of two professors at Fisk University, John W. Work, Jr., and his brother, Frederick J. Work. These men were pioneers in the preservation and development of the spirituals.

Regardless of race, the African American spiritual contributes a depth of Christian experience that is needed within the whole family of believers. We grieve that crucifixion happened to One so perfect, but we worship in praise and thankfulness for Jesus' sacrifice for our salvation.

Lord Jesus, I bow in humble adoration at the foot of your cross. Amen.

Were you there when they crucified my Lord?
Were you there when they crucified my Lord?

Refrain: Oh! sometimes it causes me to tremble, tremble, tremble.
Were you there when they crucified my Lord?

African American spiritual

50. What a Friend We Have in Jesus

"In this world you will have trouble. But take heart! I have overcome the world." (John 16:33, NIV)

The poem was short and simple. It has become one of the cornerstones of gospel truth for Christians all over the world, stating that a personal friendship with God is possible because of Jesus Christ. Poet Joseph Scriven had such a relationship. Tragedy touched his life many times, but God's strength sustained him.

Born in Ireland in 1819, his dream of service in the military abruptly ended because of his poor health. However, he was able to complete Trinity College in Dublin, Ireland, where he began a teaching career.

Wedding plans were soon in progress with his childhood sweetheart. But the day before the wedding, she was thrown from her horse into a lake and drowned.

Discouragement sent him to a new land in 1844 at age twenty-five. In Canada he became the tutor for a family in Port Hope, Ontario. But in 1855, grief entered his life again with the death of the second woman he planned to marry.

Several years later, when he received news from Ireland of his mother's illness, he wrote her of his love and prayers for her recovery. In the letter he enclosed a little poem of encouragement, "What a Friend We Have in Jesus."

One day while visiting Scriven, a friend saw the piece of paper on which the twelve-line poem was written. The friend asked, "Who wrote these beautiful words?" The humble author replied, "The Lord and I did it between us."

Composer Charles Converse was inspired by the dynamic faith expressed in the words and, in 1868, wrote the memorable tune loved by millions.

The words of this hymn are a testimony to the undying faith of a quiet Christian man; Joseph Scriven never preached great sermons, but lived his life as one. He overcame obstacles of grief, disappointment, and loneliness because of his eternal friendship with Jesus. After his death in 1886, the people he served and loved in Ontario erected a monument in his memory. His hymn is inscribed on this monument. The closing words reveal Joseph Scriven's serenity and security: "In his arms he'll take and shield thee; thou wilt find a solace there."

Lord God, to know you as a Friend who loves me, listens to me,
and leads me into real life is awesome. In Jesus' name. Amen.

What a friend we have in Jesus, all our sins and griefs to bear!
What a privilege to carry everything to God in prayer!
O what peace we often forfeit, O what needless pain we bear,
all because we do not carry everything to God in prayer.

Joseph M. Scriven, ca. 1855

51. WHEN I SURVEY THE WONDROUS CROSS

"May I never boast of anything except the cross of our
Lord Jesus Christ." (Gal. 6:14*a*)

The music of Isaac Watts was creating quite a controversy.
He readily expressed the unrest in his soul about the music of
the church, which he said was "the part of worship most closely related to heaven. But its performance among us is the
worst on earth."

He wrote the contemporary music of his day (1674–1748)
and was also considered by some to be a rebel. He was a minister in a Dissenting Congregational church. His deep faith
flowed into the music he composed, which expressed feeling
and experience. Throughout his lifetime, he composed more
than six hundred hymns. They were all extremely different
from the Psalms that were sung directly from the Bible.

The best example of his unique music is the hymn "When
I Survey the Wondrous Cross." It has been labeled the greatest
hymn in the English language. It gives an intimate look at
Jesus as he hangs on the cross and compels one to stand in
awe of such deep love that would suffer such agony. The third
stanza demonstrates this: "See from his head, his hands, his
feet, sorrow and love flow mingled down."

Author William J. Reynolds says: "Rather than using an
expected adjective such as 'cruel,' 'tragic,' or 'rugged,' Watts

describes the cross as 'wondrous.' Such graphic language reminds us that an instrument of cruel torture and death became God's wondrous instrument for our salvation."

The confused disciples did not know about God's "wondrous instrument" when Jesus told them of his future suffering and death. Peter expressed his sadness: "God forbid it, Lord! This must never happen to you" (Matt. 16:22*b*). But Jesus in anguish rebuked him, saying, "You are setting your mind not on divine things but on human things" (Matt. 16:23*b*).

Years ago when I had a wound in my side after surgery, a nurse came to my home each day to change the bandage. It was painful, but I knew the cleansing must be done to ensure proper healing. One day my friend Rochelle was there when the nurse came. The procedure began and tears flowed from my eyes. I held tightly to Rochelle's hand as she sang: "I was healed by the wound in his side, yes I was healed."

Peace covered me as I imagined some of my Lord's suffering. I knew he was with me. What is my response to that beautiful, suffering love? "Love so amazing, so divine, demands my soul, my life, my all."

O Jesus, I lovingly bow in humble adoration at the foot of your cross. Amen.

When I survey the wondrous cross
on which the Prince of Glory died,
my richest gain I count but loss,
and pour contempt on all my pride.

Isaac Watts, 1707 (Gal. 6:14)

52. WONDERFUL WORDS OF LIFE

"The words that I have spoken to you are spirit and life." (John 6:63*b*)

Composer Philip Paul Bliss was born in 1838 on a farm in Pennsylvania, his chores often neglected as his musical interests took priority. After attending a singing school in Rome, Pennsylvania, he never returned to the farm. He married and began a career as music teacher, song leader, and composer.

Bliss believed that music could be an instrument used to carry the gospel message. The first composer to use the term "gospel hymn," he felt called to obey Jesus' command to "go into all the world and preach the gospel" (Mark 16:15). Bliss preached through his music. One of his hymns that has gone into all the world is "Wonderful Words of Life." He wrote both words and music in 1874. In the three verses of the hymn, the phrase "wonderful words" appears ten times. There is no doubt that the words of the Bible were wonderful to Bliss. The second stanza describes these words: "all so freely given, wooing us to heaven."

Bliss went to his heavenly home when he was only thirty-eight years old. In 1876 he and his wife, Lucy, traveled by train to Chicago to join an evangelistic meeting at Moody Tabernacle, where he was to be the song leader. As the train crossed a ravine, the bridge collapsed, sending the passengers seventy feet below. Bliss survived the fall but as he crawled back into the wreckage to rescue his beloved wife, it burst into flames. He died with her.

But the music of Philip Bliss continues to go into all the world as millions of Christians have been inspired by his gospel songs for over a century. Each time I sing "Wonderful Words of Life," I am reminded of the importance of being a student of the Bible. To study it is to love its message. As we study Genesis through Revelation, we grow in our understanding of God's presence, purpose, and plan.

O God, thank you for the magnificent power in your Word. Amen.

Sing them over again to me, wonderful words of life;
let me more of their beauty see, wonderful words of life;
words of life and beauty teach me faith and duty.

Refrain: Beautiful words, wonderful words, wonderful words
of life.
Beautiful words, wonderful words, wonderful words of life.

Philip P. Bliss, 1874